James McSherry

Father Laval, or, The Jesuit missionary: A tale of the North American Indian

James McSherry

Father Laval, or, The Jesuit missionary: A tale of the North American Indian

ISBN/EAN: 9783741158124

Manufactured in Europe, USA, Canada, Australia, Japa

Cover: Foto ©Andreas Hilbeck / pixelio.de

Manufactured and distributed by brebook publishing software
(www.brebook.com)

James McSherry

Father Laval, or, The Jesuit missionary: A tale of the North American Indian

FATHER LAVAL;

OR, THE

JESUIT MISSIONARY:

𝔄 𝔗𝔞𝔩𝔢 𝔬𝔣 𝔱𝔥𝔢 𝔑𝔬𝔯𝔱𝔥 𝔄𝔪𝔢𝔯𝔦𝔠𝔞𝔫 𝔍𝔫𝔡𝔦𝔞𝔫𝔰.

BY

JAMES McSHERRY, Esq.,

AUTHOR OF "A HISTORY OF MARYLAND," "WILLITOFF," ETC.

BALTIMORE:

PUBLISHED BY JOHN MURPHY & CO.

182 BALTIMORE STREET.

1873.

THIS LITTLE STORY WAS DEDICATED

TO A

𝔎ind and 𝔄ffectionate 𝔉ather,

AND IS NOW

INSCRIBED TO HIS MEMORY

BY A

𝔊rateful 𝔖on.

iii

PREFACE.

THE intention of the writer of the following tale has been to portray, at least indistinctly, one of those magnificent scenes in which the Jesuits of the Canada missions were actors, in the early settlement of that country. The sufferings of the missionary, his indomitable courage in the apostolate, and the effect of Christianity upon the Indian convert, are the principal points of the picture which he has desired to present, though he has not dared to enter into all the terrible details of the Mohawk torture, as it was too often endured by those patient and heroic martyrs. The foundation of the story is laid upon the history of

Father Isaac Jogues; though the rescue in the narrative is entirely fictitious, yet its general bearing is not at variance with the results of his adventures.

Since its first issue, this story has received the compliment of a republication in England, and has obtained the favorable notice of the Catholic press of this country.

It has been for some time out of print, and having been revised and enlarged, the Publishers take pleasure in again offering it to the public in a new and more inviting dress.

CONTENTS

FATHER LAVAL.

CHAPTER I.

THE MISSIONARY.

IN the year of our Lord 1642 the various missionary stations of the Jesuits throughout Canada, or New France, as it was then called, were threatened with all the wild fury of the savage and untamable Iroquois. The Five Nations had proved themselves the most unconquerable in their hostility to the white man, to the religion which he taught, and the civilization which he endeavored to introduce. In vain had overtures of peace been made. For a time, perhaps, as if slumbering from indolence or exhaustion, they ceased to ravage, but it was

only to break forth again with more furious energy.   Their bands of braves "ranged the illim-
itable forests," with no power to control them,
and no rivals whom they dreaded.   They traversed the St. Lawrence and lakes Erie and Ontario, and they struck their enemy upon the
shores of Lake Champlain.

Every missionary on his way to his distant
station was in constant danger of captivity and
death; and yet never were those stations left
unfilled for want of brave and devoted men to
dare all the terrors of the route, and the chances
of enduring the torture at the villages of the
Mohawks.   The path to the Huron missions was
perhaps more completely beset than any other,
for the Iroquois had succeeded in cutting off, or
at least in interrupting, the communication between Upper and Lower Canada.   They had
possession of the intermediate passes.

In Quebec, in that year, the feast of St. Ignatius, the founder of the Society of Jesus, was
celebrated with no ordinary splendor.   The fathers on that joyous occasion offered up with full
hearts the glorious crown of souls, gathered from

the wilderness — gathered up to the "greater honor of God" by the sons of St. Ignatius, from the wandering children of the forest. It was no feeling of earthly glory or of human pride that swelled within their hearts as they raised them up towards heaven, throbbing high with exultation. It was not the triumph which lightens up the eye of the worldly conqueror and curls his lip, that made their step more stately, and their pale features glow with an unwonted flush. They were spiritual soldiers; and they felt, in their hearts, the glory of their calling, and the martial joy of victory over the infernal enemy against whom they battled. Many a full, deep voice trembled as it chanted the solemn service; age prayed with its chastened calmness; youth vowed to make itself more worthy of the glorious founder under whose banners they were enlisted in the service of God. Deep was the feeling that pervaded all hearts on that memorable festival.

Among the priests who knelt at the altar, was one remarkable for his worn and sunburnt aspect. A little beyond the full prime and strength of manhood, with the nobility of nature stamped

upon his brow, he was a man calculated to strike
the attention of all who looked upon him.   And
yet there was nothing hard or stern in those
grave, calm features; they were the true picture
of a good and gentle heart, a mind tutored in the
patient and enduring school of Xavier and Loy-
ola, a will subdued and mortified.   Father Jean
Laval was preparing himself for a renewal of his
arduous mission in the western wilderness.   A
few weeks of rest and relaxation had elapsed
since he had completed the perilous voyage from
the missions at the falls of St. Mary, between
lakes Huron and Superior, and now he was
assisting for the last time for many months, it
might be for ever, with his brethren of Quebec,
at the holy mystery of the altar.   And yet the
perilous voyage before him did not appear to
weigh upon his mind.   Abstracted from all
earthly things, his soul seemed only the more
closely wrapt in the contemplation of things
heavenly.   Not so with many a full heart in
that thronged temple of God: but the fulness of
their hearts only made them mingle more fervently with their prayers the name of him on

whom their eyes now rested with such deep love
and admiration. He was going once more to
that nation of pious Indians of whom they had
heard such joyful tidings—who clustered to the
true altar of God in thousands; a Christian people in the wilderness. He was going to enlarge
the empire of the gospel, to plant the cross in
new regions, to face new dangers, it might be to
win a martyr's crown. It was a noble spectacle to them, a spectacle of Christian, chivalric
devotion.

At length the last chant of the solemn mass
had ceased to swell in the crowded aisle; the
benediction had been given, and, silently and
with holy recollection, the worshippers departed
to their homes. A small group of Indians alone
remained before the church. In a few moments
Father Laval, in his cassock, accompanied by
another priest of his order, issued from the
sacristy, where he had disrobed, and advanced
towards them.

"My dear children," he said, "all my
arrangements are completed: we will depart to-
morrow. Our Superior so wills it."

2

"It is good," replied one of their number, who appeared to be the chief of the party. "Ahasistari hears his father, the blackgown."

" At daybreak, then, sachem —"

" The Hurons will be ready." And the party separated, Father Laval and his companion pursuing their walk to the house of their Order.

" Ah, my friend, what a glorious lot is yours! You go to carry the cross of Christ to the heathen! Oh! shall we not envy you the inestimable happiness of being thought worthy of such high honor?" fervently exclaimed the companion of Father Laval.

" No, my brother; rather pray for me that my unworthiness may not render fruitless the prayers of the good and pious in behalf of the benighted Indian. And yet it is a glorious field of labor; so rich, so sweet, so full of consolation; all its toils and dangers well repaid by the happy privilege of winning souls to God."

" And happy are the auspices, Father Laval! On this festival of our great saint, you prepare to add new glory to his name on earth, by bringing new children to the fold of Christ."

"And to-morrow, Father Anthony, to-morrow is the feast of '*the chains of St. Peter.*'"

"Happy coincidence, my brother," exclaimed Father Anthony. "You go on that day forth to bind the savage in the chains of Peter, to win wandering children to the footstool of his Master.'"

"Or to wear my chains like him; but, alas! I am not deserving of such favor. I shall not be deemed worthy of suffering for him who died for me. Oh, happiness! oh, bliss! I dare not hope for thee!"

"Happy apostle! happy in the chains and suffering you may be worthy of enduring. We, thy brethren, seek a remembrance in thy prayers."

"Father Anthony Daniel," said the missionary, slowly and thoughtfully, as they reached the end of their walk, "it shall be thine next."

CHAPTER II

THE DEPARTURE.

ON the following morn, the first day of August, a gallant fleet of war canoes floated gayly from beneath the guns of Fort Quebec. The plumed and painted Indians, bowing their strength to the paddles, sent their light and graceful barks rapidly into the mid-waters of the broad St. Lawrence. The sun was just rising, and breaking dim and red through the heavy mists that overhung the river; yet ere the last canoe swept into the line, the veil of vapor began to disappear before its powerful rays. Breaking into light clouds, it rose and floated slowly away towards the south, while streams of sunshine poured brightly through each opening, lighting up the earth with a rich glow, and clothing the placid bosom

of the river with a robe of gold. As the mist
dispersed, the scene around became distinct in
its full beauty, and the infant city seemed to
waken up to life and activity. A crowd of
citizens stood upon the quay, gazing eagerly
and fondly on the receding fleet, as if it contained some dear object upon which, perhaps,
they might be looking for the last time.

In the rearmost and largest canoe were the
only two white men of the party — Father
Jean Laval and his young assistant, the novice,
Rene Bourdoise. Guiding the canoe in which
they sat, Ahasistari, the chief, seemed to guard
their comfort and convenience as the first object
of his care.

The vigorous arms of the Indian rowers
impelled the canoes westward up the St. Lawrence, and when the foremost was about disap-
pearing to the view of the party on the quay,
Father Laval arose in the trembling bark, and
extending his hands towards heaven, invoked
again that blessing upon their pilgrimage,
which he had already, in company with his
brethren and whole people, so earnestly besought.

2 * B

Then, with an affectionate wave of his hand, he bade adieu to his distant friends, and resuming his seat, bowed his head in silent prayer. At the same instant a wreath of smoke, accompanied with a bright flash, burst from the walls upon the heights of Abraham, and the heavy sullen roar of cannon swept in a moment more across the waters, while the cloud of smoke rose slowly and spirally towards the heavens. Father Laval raised his head and gazed for a single instant upon the standard of France, as it waved over the impregnable fortress, and then resumed his prayer and meditation. No sound now broke upon the ear but the slight splash of the paddle as it dipped lightly but vigorously in the stream, and the murmuring of the rippling current around the sharp bow of the canoe in its rapid course.

The young novice looked upon the bright, glad scene around him with a subdued pleasure, now curiously watching the lithe and active forms of the graceful Indians as they bent their strength to their paddles, and now casting his eye towards the glorious scenery that bordered on the St. Lawrence. Perhaps scarce twenty summers had he numbered, and yet he seemed already to have drank in the severe yet serene lessons of the Jesuit school of endurance. Parting from the midst of civilized men, going unarmed and defenceless through paths waylaid by a remorseless enemy, he exhibited no fear, no regrets; in the midst of novelty and the unequalled beauty of the view around, he permitted no extravagant sign of delight to escape his lips. He subdued the transport of his feelings into the calmness of tranquil enjoyment, and by his silence and serenity won the admiring regard of the stern warriors of the Hurons.

At length Father Laval addressed him: "Rene, my son, we have entered happily upon our arduous journey. How beautiful is this earth around us, which God has given to man for the scene of his pilgrimage. He is a good God, my children, infinitely loving: if he has thus cared for our happiness here, in this sojourn on earth, what has he not prepared for the faithful and persevering servant in heaven? Let us meditate upon his infinite goodness, and mercy,

and love. It is fitting thus to begin and conse-
crate our labors."

The Indians assented with the usual short and
subdued exclamation: and for a space no sound
was heard save the regular strokes of the paddles, while the canoe proceeded with unslackened
speed. After some time spent in meditation,
the good priest employed himself in reciting his
office, and Rene Bourdoise gazed calmly down
towards the receding towers of Quebec until he
caught the last glimpse of the lofty flag-staff
bearing the banner of St. Dennis. As the
scenery became wilder and more desolate, his
mind began to recur to the bright scenes of his
native land, and to visit once more the beautiful
and fertile plains of France. The recollection of
home and early friends, of parents and distant
kindred, came rushing upon the youth, casting a
dark and gloomy hue upon the prospects before
him. Desolation and danger seemed to deepen
round him; yet suppressing these thoughts with
a single aspiration, he placed himself under the
invocation of the Holy Immaculate Virgin, and
devoted himself without reserve to the will of God.

It was in this spirit, and with such dispositions, that the whites of the party entered on
their voyage. The Hurons were seemingly
indifferent to every thing but the comfort of
those whom they were guiding and escorting to
the hunting-grounds of their tribe; and were only
warmed into life and animation by the fervor of
their hearts when absorbed in religious exercises.
They displayed in nothing that there was danger
of assault, whilst they were prepared for any
event.

Father Laval, after some time, closed his book,
and turning towards the leader of the party,
addressed him:

"My son, what think you is the prospect of
our safely passing, by the waters, to the Huron
missions? Were it not better to land and cross
the forest towards the Ottawa?"

After a moment's pause, Ahasistari replied:
"Father, the way is long and toilsome for the
white man, and his trail is broad. The Mohawk
crosses the river, and his eye is keen. The running waters keep no trail, and the Huron canoes
are swift and easy. My father, I swear to thee

that Ahasistari will share thy fortunes whether of death or life!"

"To your skill and judgment I confide the choice of the route—the issue is in the hands of the Almighty."

CHAPTER III.

THE INSTRUCTION.

OF the Indians, who composed the escort of the missionaries, some were not yet baptized. All, however, had heard, with devout attention, the preaching of the Jesuit. They had listened to him as the messenger of wonderful tidings, and had believed. But yet the careful priest hesitated long to admit to the regenerating waters of baptism those of their number who, he feared, were not sufficiently instructed in the faith of the Catholic Church. The untaught Indian, accustomed to roam through the wilderness, with the works of God forever before his observant eyes, and with incomprehensibilities around him, unable to fathom the mysteries of nature, nay, the mysteries of his own life, felt within himself the conviction of a

23

supreme, invisible Existence. With the book of
nature open before him, and nature's voice ever
in his ear, he might well, by the dim light of his
uncultivated reason, wander into the labyrinths
of polytheism ; but it was impossible for him to
stifle or forget the instinctive belief of humanity
in the God invisible, supreme over all. The
unlettered wanderer in the boundless forests had
reached the same point of knowledge at which it
had been possible for the sage of antiquity to
arrive. He worshipped the "unknown God."
But the machinery of the universe was beyond
the power of his intellect, and he found a minor
deity in every bird and beast and fish and tree
and stone. When the Catholic missionary
preached to him of the God infinite, supreme,
eternal, filling all space, at whose will the world
and all its life and beauty had sprung into being,
and at whose will the earth again would melt
away, who was the Creator and the Lord of all,
and "in whom all things lived and moved and
had their being ;" to his unsophisticated mind,
it seemed worthy of the great Spirit which his
instinct had sought after in nature, and beyond
nature, in vain.

The piety and zeal and superior knowledge of the missionary had won him credence, and when he preached to them of the Saviour who had come upon earth, of his death and of his resurrection for the salvation of all, and unfolded to them the evidences of Christianity, they listened with reverence to his words, and cherished them in their hearts.

In his own canoe, Father Jean Laval had placed two of his neophytes for the purpose of continuing their instruction during the voyage, and Rene Bourdoise, in order that he might be schooled in the best mode of conveying knowledge to the simple-minded savage.

"Huron, dost thou know who created thee? he said, addressing the elder of the two, a warrio. of some note, whose instruction he had but lately commenced.

"The great Spirit, who made the earth and the waters and the forests," replied Haukimah.

"And, Huron, did he make the buffalo and the bounding deer?"

"Yes, father; the buffalo and the bounding deer, and all things else that live."

8

"And did he make thee and me like to them?"

"My fathers taught that the buffalo and the bounding deer departed to the hunting-ground of spirits where the warrior's shade pursued them as here on earth. It is wrong. The blackgown teacheth that the great Spirit made man like himself, and breathed his breath into his nostrils—heaven was made for the man who doeth good. The wild beast dies and perishes."

Father Jean Laval, from the foundation of this simple questioning, took occasion to explain fully and minutely, and impress deeply upon the mind of those whom he was instructing, the history of man's creation, and his destiny, his fall, and the promise of his redemption, fulfilled by the coming, the passion, and the glorious death of the Saviour of the world. He told them how man's nature became corrupt by his fall; how he became perverse through his disobedience, prone to evil, subject to all the temptations of the devil.

"It is that which makes the Iroquois cruel

and blood-thirsty," said the younger neophyte; "the spirit of evil is within him."

"As he is with all bad men, my son; as he is with you when you indulge revengeful feelings towards the Iroquois, when you would do them evil for evil. You must love those who hate you."

"Shall the Huron love the Iroquois?" exclaimed the young warrior as his eyes glistened with awakened passion, and his head was elevated in disdain; "shall the dove and hawk nestle together?"

"Is the Huron a dove in his heart?" broke in the deep stern voice of Ahasistari; "the dove is tender. The Huron brave should be bold and fearless like the eagle."

"Let the Huron be a dove in his heart," said Father Jean Laval, ere the young Indian could open his lips again; "let him be a dove in purity, in meekness, in piety, in love. Let him be the eagle of his tribe when he battles in a just and lawful cause!"

"My father has spoken well," replied the chief, in a changed and softened tone.

"Yes, my dear children, your first duty is to God, the great Spirit; your next is to your neighbor. The good Spirit created you and all men to love him and serve him, and he commands you to love one another, even your enemies; to do good to those that hate you. If the Iroquois is fierce and bad, pity him, and pray that he may become better,—that he may listen to the messengers of Christ. If you hate the Iroquois, in what are you better than he?"

"It is good," said Ahasistari, "it is like a God to forgive."

And then Father Laval proceeded to inculcate upon his hearers the virtues which were necessary to, and which adorned the Christian, showing how the principles of religion were entwined around all the ties of life, and how they were connected with and ruled every circumstance of our mortal existence. He instructed them in the rules which should govern them in their intercourse with all men, and the charity so sublime and superhuman which they should cultivate in their hearts. Thus seizing every word and every trifling circumstance, he made them the occasion and the vehicle of useful instruction, and the means of initiating them into the spirit and practice as well as the doctrines of the Catholic Church.

Occasionally, to relieve their minds and to break the continuous length of his instructions, he would interpose a prayer, and occupy himself in teaching them the responses to the litanies and the prayers of the rosary. They listened with docility, and learned with quickness the portions assigned to them, and the warriors seemed to vie with each other in acquiring that great and super-eminent knowledge which the father of the black-gown dispensed to them. Thrice a day, morning, noon, and night, the Jesuit and Rene Bourdoise the novice, in accordance with their previously adopted resolution, recited a portion of the rosary to procure, through the intercession of the mother of God, the blessings of heaven upon their mission. Ahasistari and the Catholic Indians joined in the responses with devoutness, and seemed never to weary under their labors while thus cheered with the refreshing dew of prayer.

In this pious occupation the day passed pleas-

antly and quickly round. Father Laval, each
time they landed to prepare their frugal repasts,
assembled the whole party around him, gave
them a short instruction, and, having blessed
their food, sat down on the grass with them, and
shared their frugal fare.

As night approached, Ahasistari began to look
about for a convenient spot to bivouac upon, and
at length selected a beautiful and secluded inden-
ture in the river banks, shaded by lofty trees, and
protected and rendered almost impenetrable from
the land by the thick undergrowth, reaching
some distance back from the shore. Here they
landed, and, drawing up their canoes upon the
bank, prepared to pass the night upon the
spot. After their evening meal had been dispatched, Father Laval was about to commence
an instruction or exhortation to his companions,
when Ahasistari approached him respectfully,
and said:

"My father, the Mohawk may be abroad; his
ear is quick!"

"Perhaps it is better," said Father Laval, carrying out the thought of the other, without re-

plying directly to his words; "my children, meditate in silence on what you have been taught this day and pray to God for protection, invoking the intercession of Mary our holy Mother."

Wrapping themselves in their blankets, after bending their knees in silent prayer, the Indians stretched themselves upon the ground, and soon sunk into the light and watchful sleep of men accustomed to snatch their repose in the midst of danger. The Jesuit and Rene Bourdoise did not so easily betake themselves to slumber. For the novice especially was in a situation calculated to drive sleep from his eyelids until nature should sink into unconsciousness from· exhaustion. As he lay wakeful and apprehensive, he turned his eye frequently upon the form of Ahasistari, which, in the indistinct light, was barely discernible to the steady gaze. Occasionally a bright gleam from the expiring embers would lighten up the picturesque figure of the Indian. The warrior sat at the foot of a tree, resting his head upon his hand in a careless manner, which seemed to the young novice to be the attitude of one wrapt in thought and contemplation. Ahasistari was meditating; but every outward sense was on the alert, eager to catch the slightest sound or motion on the forest or upon the murmuring river. The stars were looking down from heaven sweetly and tenderly, shedding a dim light upon the moving waters, whose broken surface reflected the countless pencils of light in myriad forms of quivering beauty. Over the deep silence of the forest, broken only by those mysterious voices of the night which render the solitude more profound, was faintly heard the murmuring of the waters on the shore; so faintly that the listening ear could scarce distinguish between the almost audible stillness of the grove and the low music of the living but unruffled stream. The air was mild and calm. It was a night to worship God in.

The hours passed, and the motionless form of the watching Indian seemed to the dull and closing eye of the novice to swell into gigantic size, and then to shrink and fade away to nothingness until, in the imperceptible sinking of his senses under fatigue and slumber, the beauteous scene around him passed from before his closed orbs, and his spirit began to wander in the sunny fields of his own dear France.

How long he slept he knew not, but he was at length aroused by the hand of the Indian upon his shoulder. It was not yet day, but every preparation had already been made to depart, and the kindness of the chief had permitted the young man to enjoy unbroken, until the last moment, the deep and refreshing slumber which had wrapped his senses. Leaping up from his hard couch, the young novice performed his morning devotions, and, having made his ablution in the running waters, was ready to take his seat in the canoe the moment it was launched. Father Laval had resolved that Rene Bourdoise and himself should occupy different canoes during the rest of the voyage in order that the young man might be employed as well as himself in instructing the catechumens, of whom, as we have already said, there was a number not yet fully prepared scattered throughout the fleet. In a few moments the dark forms of the canoes shot out from the banks of the river, keeping within the verge of the heavy shadows of the overhang-

C

ing woods, and pursuing their course rapidly and silently towards the new fort of Montreal. Ere the day dawned, they had proceeded many miles upon their journey, when, striking deeper into the current, the canoes drew out in a more extended line, and continued on their course.

CHAPTER IV.

NIGHT UPON THE WATERS.

SEVERAL days were happily passed in this manner, and, although the progress of the party had been regular, the declining sun of the fourth day found them still distant from the sheltering walls of Montreal. As they were now in the most dangerous portion of their passage between the two forts, it was determined not to land, but to continue their voyage during the night; the Indians relieving each other at the paddle, and snatching a moment's repose, while the canoes proceeded slowly, and with diminished force, up the river.

Stretching themselves upon the bottom of the canoes, Father Laval and Rene Bourdoise prepared to sleep, having committed themselves to the keeping of God. The novice had already

35

become in a manner accustomed to the novelty
of his situation, and its danger from familiarity
began to lose the terror which' it had at first
possessed.

Sleep soon closed his eyes, for his heart was
pure, and he had learned to look on death too
long in the stern training of the Christian soldier
to dread his approach, come apparelled as he
might.

Ever reflecting upon life, the Jesuit is taught
to look to its last end, to value it as a means,
worthless in itself, priceless when laid down to
purchase immortal bliss. Death has no pangs
for him; for him it can not sever any earthly
ties; the only tie that binds him to this earth
leads through the portals of the tomb to heaven.
Those gates, to most men so dark and gloomy,
are but the triumphal arch through which he
shall pass when the victory over sin and hell is
won for him. Constant meditation has cooled
his passions, stemmed their rapid flow, and
taught him well the utter worthlessness of
earthly pride and pleasures and possessions.
He follows the command of the Saviour to the

youth who sought the rule of perfection. He strips himself of earthly riches. He is ready then to go forth upon the world, without staff or scrip or raiment, to do God's work, prepared for life or death, in obedience to the will of his divine Master.

Calmly and sweetly, trusting in the loving care of the mother under whose powerful intercession he had placed himself, the novice slept the sleep of youth. Soft tones, old and fond remembrances, kind voices and familiar names seemed once more to mingle in his slumbering sense, with the light murmur of the rippling wave and the low music of the zephyr that fanned his cheek. Dear faces beamed upon him. He sat again beside the well-worn and familiar hearth, and his gray-haired father smiled once more upon the son he loved, the son of his old age vowed to the service of his God. For such was the youthful Rene: from childhood dedicated to the altar, breathing the pure atmosphere of its unpolluted precincts, conscious even in his father's house and in his early years of the solemn duty which lay before him for his future life. Sweetly came the recollection

4

of his childhood's home, and those dear old faces,
with their beaming smiles, melting from beneath
the frosts of years of stern study and deep holy
meditation which had schooled his heart into
higher, nobler thought, of sweeter, purer love —
love to the Father of all fathers, engrossing and
sublimating all true love in his young heart.
But now in dreams fondly.retracing many a thousand league, and many a toilsome year, the human
spirit, true to its human nature, back to its old
affections and its mortal ties went hurrying—
but not forgetful of its own heavenly destiny.   It
was pure happiness, pure infantile joy, such as in
childhood he had felt—for now it seemed to him
that once again he was a child — a thoughtless,
gay, and cheerful child — without a care, without
a fear, with no responsibility and with no feeling
but of the present moment.   The waters of the
flowing river murmured in his ear, and fancy
broke the changeless sound into some sweet old
melody once sung to him by fond maternal lips.
The light but quivering stroke of the bending
paddle, swaying the fragile bark, and its soft and
gentle motion as it cut the waters, rocked him

sweetly till he lay like an infant slumbering on its mother's breast. Thus slept the youthful novice.

Father Laval had more care upon his mind, and it was long before he gave way to the weariness that hung upon his eyelids. He felt that the critical hour had arrived ; for if the company once reached Montreal, and commenced to ascend the Ottawa, there was less danger of being attacked by a force more powerful than their own. At length he too composed himself to slumber, confiding himself to the protection of an all-seeing God.

As leader of the party, Ahasistari, insensible to fatigue when the safety of his charge might be at issue, watched all night. To the enduring nature of the Indian this was little, and his band only sought occasional repose, in order that a portion might be fresh and prepared for any event. From the bow of his canoe, which had drawn from the rear to the head of the line, the chief scanned, with keen and watchful eye, either shore of the river as they ascended. But all nature slept, and it seemed as if with nature even the fell heart of man was at rest. No mark or trace of an enemy met his eye; for even in the dim light of the stars the wondrous sense of an Indian warrior might detect the presence of his foe, and the slightest sound, the breaking of a twig might be heard in the stillness of the hour over the murmuring waters. But all things were silent, and the chief began to hope that perhaps no Mohawks were out-lying along the river, and that their passage would be made without difficulty or danger. But he did not become less watchful.

At length the dark starlit canopy began to lighten up faintly towards the east. Dim and almost imperceptible was the first precursor of the dawn, merely a lesser darkness. Thus it passed for many minutes, making the summits of the far hills sharper and more distinct, and shrouding the lower forest in deeper gloom. Gradually the view became more distinct, and a quick eye might barely trace the forms of nature. The canoes were now approaching a narrower portion of the river, and Ahasistari became more watchful than before. At length his

eye seemed to fix upon a portion of the forest
that overhung the river above them on their
route—then he raised it up towards the sky
above the woods. The scrutiny did not seem to
satisfy him, and, guiding the canoe from the
shore so as to bring the object more to the light,
he watched it as the barks moved on. The warriors in the rearward canoes observed the motion,
but with apparent indifference still urged on
their frail vessels, knowing the skill and cool-
ness of their leader. In a little while the motion
of the canoe brought the top of that portion of
the forest opposite a bright clear star, and across
its face for a single instant came a dimness like
that caused by a thin, wiry column of smoke or
vapor.

"Ugh!" exclaimed the chief, in the deep guttural tone peculiar to the Indian, and, with a
sudden motion of his paddle, he sent the canoe
whirling in towards the southern shore under the
shadows of the hills. Then, staying its progress,
he crouched close to diminish the risk of obser-
vation by any wandering eye that might be upon
the shore. His example was silently followed,
4 *

and soon the line of canoes lay within the verge
of the dark shadows, motionless and seemingly
unoccupied.   Not a question was asked: no anxiety or curiosity was manifested; the warriors
coldly and impassively awaited the motions of
their chief.

The keen eye of Ahasistari still scanned the
forest with quick and suspicious glances, when a
slight sound struck upon his ear: it seemed like
the snapping of a twig beneath a light and cautious tread.   The sound was very faint, but it
did not escape the ear of a single warrior, the
youngest and least practised.   The Jesuit, who
lay in the canoe of the leader, began to turn un-
easily in his sleep, affected by the change from
motion to rest, and his breathing seemed to grow
louder in the stillness of things around.   Ahasistari pointed with his finger to the sleeping
missionary, and Haukimah, the neophyte, stooped
down low over the good father, and gently laid
his hand upon his shoulder.   In a moment Father Laval opened his eyes with a slight start,
but the low " hist!" and the finger of the neophyte pressed upon his lips, indistinctly visible

in the gray light, immediately recalled him to
consciousness. A single glance enabled him to
catch at least a general idea of the situation of
affairs, and raising his heart in prayer, he awaited
with resignation the end, whatsoever it might be.
Similar was the awakening of Rene Bourdoise.
The young novice had sooner fallen into a deep
and refreshing slumber, and the first checking of
the speed of the canoe had startled him, and its
ceasing had aroused him. Observing the state of
preparation around him, his young French blood,
fiery yet in spite of its long training to suppress
such worldly feeling, began to glow as he thought
that the enemies of France and foes of his religion might perhaps be at that moment lying
within reach, and that battle between man and
man, in which he durst bear no part, might soon
take place before his eyes. It was not without
an effort that he succeeded in restraining these
feelings, and giving himself up to the weapons
of prayer and humiliation of spirit. A young,
bright, glowing heart had Rene Bourdoise. Watook, his pupil, who sat by his side, observed the
mental struggle of the young ecclesiastic, and

marked the sparkling of his eye, and his heart swelled with a deeper affection as he beheld the subdued workings of the noble spirit within.

" Will the young blackgown share Watook's weapons ? " he said in a low whisper ; " Watook has a keen and polished knife, and his carabine is sure—they shall be his brother's. Watook will use the weapons of his people." As he spoke, the generous young warrior drew the knife from his belt, and tendered the arms to the young novice.

A deep blush suffused the fine face of Rene Bourdoise. It was impossible to tell what feeling most predominated in the inward struggle, and sent the evidence of shame tingling to his cheek; whether was it the manhood and the spirit of flesh yet unsubdued within him, that scorned to act like a woman when the strife should come, and yet durst not receive the proffered weapons which must remain so idle in his hands; or was it a conscious shame that his demeanor, forgetful of the bearing of the Christian messenger of love and faith, had awakened in the heart of the savage such thoughts as caused his offer, when he should have been preparing with silent prayer and resignation to win his martyr's crown? He gazed upon the weapons for a moment, but the training of the novice amidst silence and contemplation, was too strong for the impulse of the passions, and putting them aside, he said:

"Keep your arms, my brother! They would be useless in my hands; I know not how to wield them. I am a man of peace. None vowed to the service of the altar may stain their hands in human blood, but must submit to the trials which are given them. Oh, my Father!" he continued mentally, "who readest all hearts, forgive the sinful thoughts which carried me away, and stirred up the evil of my nature;" and bowing down his head, he sat composed and motionless, not less the wonder than the admiration of the young man, who saw that fear had nothing to do with conduct, to him, hitherto little acquainted with the missionaries, so inexplicable.

As the canoes swung in towards the shore, impelled by an occasional stroke of the paddle, the current bore them somewhat lower down the

river. The descent was evident; for the trees
upon the bank seemed slowly to pass by them, as
it were, giving the appearance of rest to the
canoes. The Indians did not endeavor to keep
them on their former course, but permitted them
to drop gently down the stream. Father Laval
kept his eye intently fixed upon the forest; but
he found it difficult to penetrate the darkness
which shrouded it. The canoes had now reached
a point where the underwood was not so thick as
that above, and where there was little danger of
an ambush. Ahasistari again emitted a low exclamation, and pointed towards an open part of
the forest. The eye of Father Laval followed
the direction, and up the stream, in the rear of
the heavy underwood, he caught a momentary
glimpse of the dying embers of a fire. The thick
trunk of a tree in the next instant concealed it
from his sight. There was no sign of life or
motion near it or around it. He again assumed
his place at the bottom of the canoe, from which
he had raised himself to look around. The eye
of the chief was now turned upon the portion of
the forest immediately before them, and he held

a consultation in low tones with the old warrior by his side.

" Haukimah, the trail is there," he said, pointing to a spot which seemed to the Jesuit, who again raised his head as the chief spoke, to present no marks by which to distinguish it from the banks above or below it.

" Yes, the Mohawk has left it broad — a yengeese might follow in it: the Mohawk is cunning ! "

" He is a wolf, but he leaves his trail like a bear."

The old Indian shook his head doubtingly, and, after a moment's pause, replied :

" The Iroquois can hide his trail if he will ; — he is strong, he has left a broad trail."

" He is weak ; a fox making the trail of many wolves to frighten the hunter !   If he were strong he would lie hid like the panther who springs on the passing elk."

" He is not waiting for his prey : he has stricken it near the wigwams of the pale-face, and has borne it away.   He is strong and fears not pursuit ; his fire is burning out ; he has gone ; " and Haukimah pointed towards the south.

It did not seem improbable that the party of
Mohawks had passed on by that route during the
night, leaving their camp-fire behind them unex-
tinguished, and their trail so broad as to negative
the idea of an ambush at that spot; yet the chief
determined to reconnoitre more closely before he
ventured to pass onwards in front of the suspicious spot, and thus expose his party to the certainty of discovery and pursuit.

The light had already become more distinct,
and the marks about which the warriors differed
became at last visible to Father Laval himself,
though, had not his attention been directed to the
spot, he could not have discovered their existence.
The low bushes on the edge of the water were
displaced and beaten down, though portions
seemed as if carefully replaced, while the underwood above on the higher portion of the bank,
which extended upwards a few feet from the surface of the water, presented on their lower branches
bent and broken boughs and torn leaves, as if
done by the grasp of persons carelessly ascending.
The canoes still continued to near the shore, and
were kept by the occasional stroke of the paddle

from descending farther down the current. They were now within a very short distance of the bank, but it was impossible to discover there the least evidence of life or motion, and the two Frenchmen began to comfort themselves with the reflection that the Indians had departed, and that nothing was to be apprehended. The Hurons, however, were still silent and watchful, cautiously concealing as much of their bodies as they could in their canoes. The chief again turned, and spoke in a low tone to Haukimah.

"How many does my brother count upon the sand?" and he pointed to the bank at the edge of the water.

The old warrior held up three fingers.

"Yes, there were but three canoes of them," said Ahasistari; "there is nothing to fear."

Father Laval looked in wonder for indications from which the warriors had drawn their conclusion, but in vain. To the Indian they were plain enough. It seemed that the Mohawks, if Mohawks they were, had proceeded with an utter disregard of the usual precautions which Indians, especially in an enemy's country, adopted to

5   D

conceal their path. On the sand the prints of
moccasined feet were stamped deeply, but were
scarcely perceptible in the dim light; and in three
places, close together, the indentures made by
the bow of a canoe, carelessly dragged from the
water, were indistinctly seen. Whilst the two
chiefs more closely examined the shore to discover if any deception were practised upon them,
the canoe in which the novice was placed shot up
towards them, and the young Indian Watook,
uttering a hiss like that of the water-snake,—so
like, that Father Laval involuntarily started with
disgust at the seeming proximity of the imaginary
reptile,—exclaimed, "The Mohawk!"

Every eye followed the direction of his extended hand, and at the moment a dusky form
was seen darting rapidly from one tree to another,
lower down and nearer the canoes. An instant
after a wild yell broke from the forest; the flash
of rifles lit up its dark shades and gleamed upon
the waters; a cloud of arrows rattled down upon
them, and half stifled groans arose from the
canoes. Every shot came from above, none as
yet from the forest in front or below the canoes.

None was returned. Covered with dense smoke, and concealed in their coverts, the unseen foe would have suffered little from the fire of the canoes had they returned it. The moment that the yell broke out, Father Laval felt the light boat spring suddenly in the water, impelled by the powerful arms of the Hurons, who sternly and silently bent to their paddles, hoping to reach a cover, and make successful defence. The discovery, the war-cry, and the rattling volley followed each other almost instantaneously; but the impulse to the light barks had been so quick and strong that, ere the volley pealed, they had cleared half the space towards the shore. It was a fortunate movement; the rapidity of their progress had rendered the aim of their ambushed foes uncertain, with the clumsy and unsure weapons with which the Dutch of New York scantily furnished them in their trade. But the speed of the canoe began to relax, broken paddles floated in the water, and the Indians who had borne them crouched low, grasping their arms, and watching intently for some object, head, leg, or arm, to aim at. The

Jesuit felt the water slowly rising around his feet—the canoe was riddled, and was filling fast. Little better was the fate of the rest. It seemed as if the foe had aimed principally at the canoes, as if to prevent escape, and, had all their shots taken effect, they must have sunk at once.

It was a moment of intense anxiety,—death from the ambush, death from the wave, was before them and around. It was doubtful whether they could reach the shore. In the midst of danger there was one thought more painful to the Jesuit than the thought of death. There were those around him who had not yet been baptized, and with agony he reflected that each pealing shot, each hissing shaft, might send one of these unfortunate children of the forest, unwashed from the dark stain of sin, to the presence of his God. The shot that every instant whistled around him had no terrors for him: the deep responsibility of human souls was upon him.

The old warrior Haukimah sat motionless before him. His head was rested on his hand, his rifle lay across his knee—he looked steadily in the face of the priest, and marked with deep concern the pain which shot across his features. The hunting-shirt of the warrior was dripping with blood, yet no sign of pain escaped him, but a wistful glance lingered upon his face as he fixed his eyes upon the countenance of the Jesuit.

"You are wounded?" said Father Laval.

The Indian slowly and somewhat painfully bowed his head.

"And seriously — it is near your heart!" continued the priest.

"Haukimah's last fight is fought," replied the Indian patiently: "he will go to the spirit-land."

"And, alas! you have not yet been baptized."

"I have sought it — I wait!"

"Yes, it has been delayed that you might be further instructed: you have been instructed — it can be delayed no longer."

A faint smile of joy passed over the stern features of the wounded man, and their look of fixed determination relaxed into a softer expression.

"It is good," he said, quietly.

"Do you repent for all your offences against the good Spirit?"

5 *

"I have ever loved him; if I have offended, I am sorry," he said faintly.

There was no space for further questioning, and the good priest arose, his large form presenting a fair mark to the foe; heedless of danger, he stooped and filled his hand with water from the river, and pouring it upon the upraised forehead of the warrior, pronounced the holy and mystic words of the sacrament. The eye of the dying Indian again lit up—a joyous smile passed once more across his features; his lips, motionless before, opened, and faint, indistinct words of prayer escaped them. Then a gushing sound was heard; his hand moved wanderingly towards the wound—the blood was bursting from it in a dark and bubbling stream. His head sank upon his breast, and the spirit of the "regenerated" had taken its flight.

"May he rest in peace," mentally ejaculated Father Jean Laval as he cast his eye once more upon the scene around. It had now become terrific. The fragile bark was sinking beneath them; escape by the river was impossible: escape by the shore seemed already doubtful. The brave

Hurons, taken at disadvantage, were unable to display their accustomed valor. At a signal from the chief, two warriors sprang from the canoe, and thus lightened and buoyed up the sinking bark, at the same moment, almost, a few strokes sent it within fording of the land. Every man made for the shore, grasping his rifle in his left hand, while his right brandished his tomahawk. Aha-sistari bounded to the beach. Bidding Father Jean Laval to follow him, it was but a moment's work to reach a cover in the woods. He was seconded by a number of his braves, and ere the last canoe had touched the shore, the sharp crack of the Huron carabines was heard on the flank of the Iroquois. As suddenly the firing ceased. The Iroquois, surprised by the unexpected activity of the Huron movement, clung close to their coverts, and for a time a fearful and unbroken silence hung upon the scene of death.

Upon the shore, by the side of a dying Indian, knelt Father Jean Laval. The cross of Christ was in his hands, and the eyes of the departing rested on it. Words of holy comfort flowed from his lips; the solemn absolution was pronounced, and, anointed and aneled, the spirit of the Christian warrior took its flight, in the midst of the stern silence that momentarily reigned around that scene of strife, to regions where neither battle nor death can come. As the last convulsive throb of dying agony ceased, and the muscular limbs of the warrior fell back motionless from the death-struggle, the priest arose from his posture by the side of the lifeless body. "Have mercy on him, O Lord!" he said in a low, sad voice, and turned away towards the forest.

CHAPTER V.

THE CONFLICT.

ILENCE and darkness on the scene! Not a movement in the forest—not a ray of light, save the dim gray of the far-off sky—no sound but the half hushed moan of pain, jarring sadly with the soft music of flowing waters. It was a living solitude. No voices were heard where there were many ready to break forth in fury; and where there were many glowing with the flame of human passion, no forms were seen but one. That form enclosed a gentle spirit.

The Jesuit strode towards the forest.

Gloom was upon his path, but an invincible tranquillity reigned within his breast. Over the stillness, more startling by its sudden contrast with the wild peal of battle which had ceased so suddenly, came now and then the rustling of leaves, as the ambushed foes fell guardedly back, assuming new positions, and manœuvring with the cautiousness of Indian warfare. It was at the mingling of night and morning, and the fading stars looked sadly down their parting, as it were, into the soul of the dark river.

The priest pressed on, heedless or unconscious of the danger that lurked within the forest. He gained the opening of a slight ravine; as he stepped forward, an obstacle caught his foot, and he fell to the earth. Putting out his hand to raise himself, it rested upon a cap—he held it up to examine it—it was the cap of Rene the novice. A shudder passed through his frame—there was a murmur of sorrow and prayer, a sinking of the heart—but he still passed on. A few feet further lay a wounded Huron. A low sigh escaped the lips of the warrior, and he endeavored to turn himself upon the ground, but in vain. The Jesuit bent over the Indian, and, in a low whisper, asked him: "Son, hast thou been baptized?"

"No, my father!" he said, in a faint and weak voice.

The place they occupied at the bottom of the ravine was somewhat covered from the position of the Iroquois. There was yet time for Father Laval to seek cover in the rear of his Hurons, and perhaps escape would have been possible; for the Iroquois were now busily occupied in slowly and cautiously extending their forces in order to outflank, and thus drive the Christian warriors from their covers. So guarded had been the movements of both parties, and such the gloom, that, as yet, neither Huron nor Iroquois had gained an opportunity of firing with any certainty of aim, and both were too wary to throw away a shot, and, at the same time, discover their whole manœuvre to the foe by the flash of their fire-arms.

Father Laval arose and crept lightly towards the river. As he passed by a little hillock or mound, he was startled by the cracking of a twig and a low hiss like that of a serpent. Hesitating a moment, he recollected the sound he had heard in the canoe, and, reassured, fixed his eye upon the spot until he distinguished a dark object moving towards him, and slowly erecting its

head from the ground as it approached. In a
moment more Ahasistari was at his feet, and in
a low voice addressed him:

"Father, hasten; there is yet time to flee!
Follow me!"

"I can not," said the Jesuit; "there are souls
to be saved—the dying to be baptized! Flee
you, and save yourself!"

"No. Ahasistari will not flee without his
father," said the Indian, drawing himself up
proudly from the ground.

"Go, chief; you have your duties, I have
mine; the brave man does his duty, and leaves
the rest to God. Go you to yours—leave me
to mine."

"You will not follow me?"

"I dare not;" and the Jesuit pointed back to
the spot where he had left the wounded Indian.
The chieftain turned his eye towards it.

"It is not far from the end of their line! You
will do your duty. Ahasistari will do his by
your side—. Hist!" he said, suddenly interrupting himself, and raising his finger to demand
silence. Father Laval listened intently, and

discovered the light trampling of moccasined feet; then the low cry of an owl struck upon his ear, and again all was silent.

"They are gathering for a charge," said the chieftain. "Ahasistari must be there to meet them. When you hear the war-cry of the Hurons, know that your children are fighting to save you. Hasten along down the shore and seek a hiding-place." The chief stretched himself upon the ground, and was soon lost in the obscurity which still pervaded the scene.

With a rapid step the Jesuit turned towards the river, lifting up his heart to God, as he went along, for assistance in this trial. To fill his cap with water, and retrace his steps to the side of the wounded Indian, was but the work of a moment. The eyes of the warrior fastened upon the cooling liquid that oozed from the cap; and with a supplicating look, he laid his finger upon his parched and feverish lip, and uttered the single word "water." The Jesuit raised his head upon his arm, and applied the cooling draught to the sufferer's mouth. A grateful expression passed across his countenance, and

6

Father Jean laid his head once more upon the turf; and, having uttered a prayer, stretched forth his hand, about to pour upon his head the regenerating waters of baptism. At that moment a heavy grasp was laid upon his bared head, which was drawn backwards till his uplifted gaze rested upon the fierce countenance of an Iroquois, whose right hand brandished above him a scalping-knife already dripping with blood. A fiendish smile played upon the features of the savage as he paused to contemplate his work. There was time!—A moment! oh, inestimable moment! worlds could not purchase thy value. There was time. The baptismal water laved gently the brow of the dying, and the words of the sacrament arose—"O God! I thank thee—" exclaimed the Jesuit; and the knife of the savage began to descend. A single shot pealed suddenly upon the silence.

Ahasistari, the fearless chief of the Hurons, had crept back swiftly to the position of his warriors, and prepared to meet the expected onslaught of the Mohawks. With the quick and ready skill of the Indian, he determined to

entrap the foe when the assault should begin, and
had already placed himself, with a few chosen
men, stealthily in advance, in a nearer and more
favorable position, when his eye, wandering un-
easily in search of the Jesuit, rested upon the
spot where he had left him. Dimly it caught
the form of the priest, bent back by the strong
grasp of the savage, and the uplifted knife suspended. He sprang forward. To fire was to
disclose his stratagem to the foe; to desist would
be death to the priest. He sternly swung his
carbine into rest—his sinewy hands grasped it
as firmly as if the muscles had been steel. Thus
it rested for a moment, motionless; then came the
clicking of the trigger, and a cloud of smoke, with
a sheet of flame from the muzzle, swept over his
still form. The blow of the Iroquois descended:
but it was the harmless falling of the lifeless
arm—the bullet of the Huron had passed
through his heart. He fell forward heavily
upon the priest.

Out broke the fierce war-whoop of the Mohawks—shots pealed and arrows flew. Then
came the wild rush, the trampling of many feet

bursting through the forest covers, and the clash
of many weapons. Hand to hand, Mohawk and
Huron fought. The occasional flash of fire-arms
blazed around, lighting up the scene with its
lurid rays, which glanced upon the plume of the
warrior as he sprung forward to the charge and
sparkled upon his uplifted weapons, made the
waving forest-spray glow as if touched with
liquid fire, and danced madly along the rippling
waters of the dark river. Over the wild music
of battle, which man in his strength and passion
loves, came subdued the sorrowful moaning of
the wounded.

A few rapid bounds brought the Huron chief
to the side of the priest. Raising him up gently,
he said, when he saw him recovered from the
effects of the incident:

"Father, go now! Far down the bank of
the river you will find the undergrowth thick
and heavy—keep by the edge of the water. We
are outnumbered; our only hope is in flight.
The Hurons will remain while you remain.
When you have fled, we also will seek safety."

"Then I must go!" said the Jesuit, and gathering up around him the long black gown which he wore, he prepared to flee from the spot.

Ahasistari stooped down and grasped the scalp-lock of his foe, and was about to pass his knife around the skin to tear it from his head. His hand was arrested by the priest: —

"Do not violate the dead, my son!"

"He is a Mohawk, my father!"

"He is a man — you have killed him in battle — do not mutilate his body. It is not Christian."

The warrior raised himself from the body of his foe, and reverently made the sign of the cross upon his forehead; then, pointing the way to the Jesuit, bounded back to his first position amid a shower of balls and arrows that whistled around him as he emerged from the ravine. Looking back, he caught a glimpse of the form of the Jesuit hurrying down the path he had designated. In the next moment the Huron chief was in the thickest of the conflict.

Gathering new spirit from the presence of their leader, the Christian warriors still made good their position against the foe; but it was

6 *   E

evident that the struggle could not be long
protracted. Yet each moment gained served to
increase the distance between the Iroquois and
their father of the black gown. At length the
thinned numbers of his warriors gave notice to
the chief that retreat could not longer be delayed.
At the signal, the Hurons sprung back from tree
to tree, securing cover as they retired, and, bat-
tling thus each foot of ground, they made the
advance of the Mohawks slow and cautious.

Ahasistari approached a well-tried warrior and
whispered a command in his ear, — the Indian
hurried to the rear and turned towards the river.
A moment after, a little below the landing, along
the shore where the rippling waves broke in a
line of light upon the sands, a dark form seemed
to rest for a moment prostrate upon the grass,
then with a quiet motion rolled slowly down the
slope to the river's bank, and, without a single
splash, disappeared beneath the water's edge.
An upturned canoe was floating by the spot:
imperceptibly its motion appeared to quicken,
and when it had gained some distance from the
shore, it was suddenly righted and an Indian

carefully crept over the side. A yell broke from
the forest proving that he was discovered, and a
few shots whistled around him; but seizing a
paddle, which had been fastened in the canoe, he
whirled it in defiance at the foe, and then urged
his bark down the river.

At length time enough had elapsed for Father
Laval to gather a sufficient start, and his Hurons
betook themselves to flight, having selected the
spot opposite their last bivouac as the final place
of rendezvous for those who might escape. The
main band shaped their course somewhat from
the river, while Ahasistari, accompanied by a
single warrior, hastened to the spot to which he
had directed the Jesuit to proceed.

Father Laval had turned away from the scene
of strife, and was hurrying down the shore when
he heard the groan of a wounded Indian whose
strength had failed him as he crept towards the
river-bank. He paused. How could he flee?
How leave behind him so many souls to whom
his ministry was necessary? He turned from his
path; he knelt by the side of the Huron, and left
him not till the shout of the pursuers, driving

deeper into the forest, became faint upon his ear. At length he arose, and heedless of the words of the chief, retraced his steps to the now silent scene of battle. Many a time he knelt and shrived the dying Christian warrior, or baptized the departing neophyte, and uttered words of hope to the wild savage. Kindly and gently, and with almost a woman's touch, he laved the parched lips and throbbing brow of the wounded, and soothed their pains. Absorbed in this work of holy love, he heard not the approaching steps of a form that soon gained his side.

"Oh, my father, I came to seek thy body — and, joy, I find thee safe!"

"Ah! Rene, my son! heaven bless thee," said the Jesuit as he gazed affectionately upon the youth. "I believed thee dead — see, I found thy cap upon the field. I mourned for thee, my son."

"Yes, I lost it in my rapid flight. The young Indian Watook hurried me to the shore, and led me to the rear. There in safety, I watched the progress of the fight, until it became necessary for me to flee deeper into the woods. Making a detour as the foe went off in pursuit, I came hither to seek thee."

· "It is well: we will die together, comforting each other."

"If it be the will of Providence, my father." And the Jesuit and the novice betook themselves to their office of love.

A young Iroquois warrior, wounded severely but not fatally, had fainted from loss of blood. He now began to revive; and an involuntary groan broke from his lips. Rene Bourdoise raised his head from the ground, whilst the Jesuit endeavored to stanch the wound. The effusion had been great, and if it continued longer would prove fatal. No mean surgeon was Father Jean, and he worked with a charitable heart. Whilst the two Frenchmen were thus engaged, the loud shouts of the returning Mohawks broke upon their ears. The savages had observed the escape of the Huron in the canoe, and, fearing that succor might be near, dared not protract the pursuit too long. Redoubled yells of joy came forth as they caught a glimpse of the two most highly prized of their foes, whose escape

they had feared. Bounding forward, two warriors were about to grapple with them; they
came with uplifted arms, but the Jesuits, unmoved, continued to perform their charitable
labors. Father Jean had just succeeded in
stanching the flow of blood, and was smooth-
ing down the bandage that compressed the
wound; Rene Bourdoise laved the brow of the
Iroquois.

The two warriors stood still, astonished, and
then, uttering the deep, low guttural exclamation
peculiar to their race, their only expression of
surprise, dropped their arms, and, turning, gazed
on one another in unmingled wonder. They
were soon joined by their companions, who gathered near by this scene so new to them, and the
same low exclamation ran around the group.
In sooth it was an unwonted contrast: man the
fiend, and man the angel;—the warrior, red with
blood, smoking with slaughter; and the priest,
calm and passionless, breathing peace and charity
to all men, binding up the wounds of his enemy.
Father Jean arose, with his arms crossed upon
his breast, his benign features glowing with a

holy enthusiasm. The priest and the savage stood face to face. The dark flashing orb of the warrior slowly yielded to the softening influence of the mild and gentle eye of the Jesuit; suddenly he turned away his glance and approached the wounded man, he laid his hand upon his brow, as if to discover that there was no deception. Then he coldly watched the face of the sufferer. The novice still supported his head, and laved his brow and lips. In a moment more the wounded man opened his eyes, and a faint smile played across his features.

"Good, Kiskepila!" muttered the Mohawk chief, and turned away.

Father Jean had now time to look about him, for he was left unmolested. The Mohawks had made several prisoners in the pursuit, whom, six in number, some of the conquerors had just dragged up, bound tightly and securely. In an hour more the last straggling pursuer had returned, the dying Hurons had been scalped and tomahawked, the bodies of the fallen Iroquois buried, and the conquerors and their prisoners, marching in single file and with a party in advance, bearing their wounded upon litters made of boughs, left the banks of the St. Lawrence where they had concealed their canoes, and struck off deep into the forest, towards the Mohawk villages.

CHAPTER VI.

THE MORN.

THE sun came up over the eastern hills, brightly and beautifully, not a cloud across his path. His first slanting beams fell upon the form of a tall warrior, stealing his way down the banks of the St. Lawrence; a short distance behind came another, cautiously covering and concealing every footstep as he passed, while to the south, deep in the forest, might be heard the sounds of conflict and pursuit. Rapidly they hurried on, yet carefully, until at length the underwood became thick and heavy, and difficult to penetrate, and the ground soft and swampy. Then, emerging from the wood, they kept along by the edge of the water, searching closely for the marks of footsteps upon the sand or clay. The examination was in vain.

For a moment the tall warrior looked about in doubt; then, renewing the scrutiny, proceeded down the river. But he met with no better success. An unusual expression of pain passed across his features, and, resting the butt of his gun upon the ground, he leaned upon it in thought. His dress was torn and bloody, and the marks of many wounds were upon him. The sun played brightly across the face of Ahasistari, but his spirit was dark and sad. He had found no trace of Father Laval. His solemn vow was in his memory.

At length twice he whistled, low, but piercingly; at the second time a rustling was heard a short distance down the bank where the bushes overhung the water, and lifting carefully aside the leafy branches, a Huron appeared, urging his canoe from his hiding-place. A few strokes sent the light bark to the feet of Ahasistari, and the rower stood beside him. The three Indians spoke together for a moment, and then sat down silently upon the shore. A slight noise startled them, and Ahasistari exclaimed, "He comes!" In a moment more a step was heard upon the

sand, and Watook, soiled and stained with the
marks of battle, stood before them. He looked
Ahasistari in the face, and then his head sunk
down upon his breast in silence. The chief
addressed him:

"Speak, Huron!"

Raising his hand towards the south, while his
eyes glowed like burning coals, the young brave
exclaimed: "The Hawk carries off the dove;
the Mohawks lead away the father of the black
gown and the young Frenchman to their villages,
to the torture: and Watook"—and his strained
arms pressed tightly against his bosom, as if
to keep down its inward struggle—"Watook
looked upon it."

Ahasistari sat motionless for a moment, then
looked fixedly at the young Indian, his eye seeming to pierce into the depths of his soul. Not a
muscle moved; not a nerve quivered; but there
was a sorrowful sternness in his glance. Then
he gazed around upon the group of Hurons:

"How many Iroquois? The days are many
before the villages can be reached—and night
and day—" and he grasped his knife express-

ively. A deep exclamation of approval broke
from his two companions. Watook replied not,
but pointed to the sands of the shore, and then
to the leaves of the forest.

"It is useless," said the chief, and sunk again
into silence. At length, raising himself up to his
full height, he said : " I have sworn, my brothers !
you are bound by no vow. Go ! the waters are
open to Quebec. Ahasistari will join his father
of the black gown, and share his fate."

The Hurons drew back from the shore to the
side of their chief, and stood immovable. A
gleam of hope broke upon the mind of the leader,
and, pointing to Watook, he said : " Go ! sweep
down the river to the place of gathering ; bring
up the warriors who may have escaped, and lead
them upon our trail ; we will rescue our people,
or perish with them."

Watook's heart beat high. He would bring
rescue to the very villages of the Mohawks, and
save the novice and the priest. He stepped
lightly into the canoe, and, with a few strokes,
sent it far into the current. Then waving his
hand to the three Hurons who stood silently

gazing after him, he steered his course directly down the river.

"Watook hath a bold young heart; he will lead the braves of the Hurons when the arm of Ahasistari is cold," said the chief; and the three devoted warriors turned away upon the trail of the enemy. . . . . .

The Iroquois marched silently on through the pathless forest, striking directly for their villages, guided only by that wonderful instinct which enables an Indian to toil on, day and night, over hill and valley, through forest and thicket and swamp, as unerringly as if directed by the compass. The prisoners were placed in the centre of the line, and so guarded that escape was impossible. The two Frenchmen, like the Hurons, were bound tightly with thongs of deer-skin, but, in the midst of their sufferings, they enjoyed the happy privilege of being together.

The hour of noon had come; the heat was oppressive even in the shaded forest, and the thick black dresses of the Jesuit and the novice increased the sufferings of their painful march. At length the party paused to refresh themselves.

7 *

"Rene, my son," said Father Laval, "let us offer up the second part of the rosary. It is the five dolors. The recollections it contains will console us in our sufferings. In our misfortunes we must pray to God to assist us with his heavenly consolations, and to enable us to endure them with patience. Let us offer them up as an atonement through the blood of Christ for our past offences."

The novice acquiesced in silence, and the priest began the prayers. For a moment their captors did not heed the conversation of the prisoners. Father Laval proceeded, and Rene Bourdoise said the responses. Hitherto the captive Hurons had maintained a stern and dogged silence, permitting no sign of pain to escape them, and enduring, passively and with native stoicism, all the insults of the Mohawks. But the sound of the first "Ave Maria," in the clear voice of the Jesuit, came like sweet music to their sullen hearts, softening their savage humor, and soothing them into love and prayer. Gently its holy influence spread among the group of sufferers, and their stern features became first sad, then

calm and placid, until the light of religious aspiration beamed from many a scarred face turned
mildly up to heaven. The response came low
and broken from the lips of the young novice,
swelling up, like a sweeping wave, as one by one
the deep musical tones of the captive Hurons
joined it. *"Ave Maria!"* it came like the
thought of a loving mother, like the memory
of a holy love. *Ave Maria!* swelling up, in the
wild forest, from captive hearts, from parched
and feverish lips, calmed by its gentle murmurs,
to the mother of the sorrowful, the mourning.
Ave! like dew to the withering flower, was the
sweet prayer to the stricken soul, and tears came
down the swarthy cheeks of the Christian warriors.

Amazed, the Mohawks looked upon the scene;
then they laughed aloud contemptuously at the
faint-hearted braves who wept—*wept* in captivity.

"Dogs! women!" they said; "are the Hurons
no warriors? Shall we go back to their tribes
to carry off a brave to torture? Ye are women!
our squaws will beat you with whips! Ye are
not worthy of a warrior's death."

But the Christian Hurons prayed on—*Sancta Maria!*—their full, deep voices piercing up to heaven, heedless of the scorn and taunts and blows of their captors. At length a Mohawk approached the Jesuit.

"Does the word of the Medicine turn the Huron warriors to women? He is a magician— let him be silent;" and he struck him a blow in the face with his clenched hand. The blood gushed from the lips of the priest, and he bowed his head in silence. . . . . .

In the forest from a thicket three figures, crouching low, glared fiercely out upon the scene; over the dark features of the chief of these flashed the fire of anger; his nostrils were dilated, his lips parted, his hand grasped his carabine convulsively. Then as the priest bowed meekly to the blow, the warrior released his weapon and pressed his hands upon his brow as if to shut out the scene; a low sigh escaped him, and he too knelt and prayed. But for the meek bearing of the priest, recalling the duty of the Christian to the heart of the chief, there surely would have been death among the conquerors

in that instant. Ahasistari knelt and prayed.
The time for action had not yet come: it was
not vengeance, but deliverance that he sought.

The Jesuit bowed meekly to the blow; then
raising his eyes up to heaven, while his arms
were drawn back by the tight thong around his
wrists, he prayed on in silence. In silence prayed
the captives — but the still incense of their hearts
floated upwards not lest sweetly to the throne of
God. It was the dedication of the forests of the
Iroquois to the faith of Christ.

The Mohawks soon made their repast, and
snatched a few moments of repose. The wretched
remains of their dinner were thrown to the captives, whose hunger was left unsatisfied, while,
from the tightness of their bands, they were
unable to enjoy the momentary rest afforded by
the halt. The line of march was soon formed
again, and the Mohawks, refreshed by their
repose, hurried on the tired captives at a rapid
pace, urging the weary and the lagging with
heavy blows. Many hours passed thus.

Rene Bourdoise was faint and weary, and his
faltering step betokened that without rest his

F

strength would soon give out. In that case a
certain death awaited him; for the captors would
not pause or delay when a blow of the tomahawk could, in a moment, relieve them of their
trouble.

A Mohawk warrior, perceiving his weariness,
approached him, and, brandishing his weapon
over his head, pointed forward to the route they
were pursuing, and intimated, by a significant
gesture, his fate in case he should be unable to
keep up with the party. Thus incited, the young
novice exerted himself anew, and, ever and anon,
his tormentor, as his efforts seemed to flag, assumed
a threatening posture, or struck him with a heavy
stick which he had picked up on the march, or
pricked him forward with the point of his knife.
The folds of his black robe were stiff with blood,
yet the fainting novice toiled on patiently, turning
up his eyes to heaven, and murmuring a gentle
prayer for his tormentors. Father Laval, stronger
and more accustomed to fatigue, looked in helpless agony upon the suffering of his young companion; he cheered him onward with words of
hope, and then, as the cruelty of the savage

increased, he consoled him with thoughts of holy comfort.

"Bear up, my son. Thou art the soldier of Jesus. Thou art scourged—*He* was scourged. It is a glorious privilege to die in his service; heaven is the reward of the happy martyr."

"Pray for me, father, pray for me. O God!" continued the youthful novice, looking sadly up to heaven, "O God! grant me strength to endure this trial; grant me fortitude!"

The road became more difficult and the progress more painful. A powerful Huron marched near the delicate young Frenchman; no word had yet escaped his lips. At length he approached the sufferer, and, pressing his huge shoulder against him, said:

"Lean on me, my brother!"

At the same moment Kiohba, the relentless Mohawk, again pricked the bleeding novice with his knife. The youth started forward, and, with a deep groan, fell to the ground. There he lay, unable to rise. The Iroquois grasped his tomahawk with a savage exclamation, and raised it over his head to strike the exhausted captive.

It was a moment of agony. The tall Huron sprang forward; with a mighty effort he burst the cords that bound his wrists, and rushed between the Iroquois and his victim. On his left arm he caught the descending blow, which gashed deep into his brawny muscles; with his right he lifted up the light form of the novice, and, folding it to his powerful chest, while the pale face of the insensible youth rested gently on his dark-red shoulder, strode sternly forward to the front of the group of captives. Deep exclamations of satisfaction escaped the Iroquois; but no one attempted to interrupt the warrior, for the Indian loves a bold deed.

"He is brave," said one; "he is worthy of the stake."

"Yes, he is a warrior; he shall die by the torture!"

The Huron strode on with his helpless burden, as tenderly and gently guarding it as a father does the child he loves.

"Le Loup will bear his young white brother," he exclaimed.

Tears flowed down the cheeks of the Jesuit,

and he raised his heart to heaven in thankfulness
for the providential rescue of his companion.

At the same instant the cry of a hawk was
heard in the forest, repeated thrice clearly and
shrilly, then seeming to die away in the distance
—a gleam of joy broke out on the bronzed face
of the Huron, and with a firmer and lighter step
Le Loup pressed onward. He knew by the
signal that his chief was upon their trail, and
that three of his tribe were near. The Iroquois
listened suspiciously to the sound, but it was
repeated no more. . . . . .

The sun was sinking low in the west. The
shades of the hills grew out lengthening. On the
bosom of the river the red light fell in streams,
sparkling from the summits of the little waves.
Far down its waters, many a weary mile, a war
canoe, urged on by a single Indian, made its way.
Large drops of sweat stood upon the rower's
brow. A moment he paused and gazed upon
the setting sun, then, shaking his clenched hand
towards the far southwest, bent sternly to his
oar once more.

At length he turned the bow of his canoe
8

towards the shore; he reached it, and bounded
on the beach. Then drawing his bark upon the
sand, he stepped into the forest with his tomahawk in his hand, and began to examine the
trees some distance from the water, and, finding
no marks on them, notched several in a peculiar
manner. As he went further in, a figure stepped
from behind a large oak which had hitherto concealed him, and approaching the canoe, inspected
it carefully, and afterwards bent over the footsteps of the young Indian. The person was
dressed in a hunting-shirt gathered close around
his waist by a leathern belt, which also served to
support a long curved knife and a small steel
axe. A large powder-horn and a ball-pouch of
deer-skin were slung over his shoulder; his feet
and legs were protected by moccasins and leggings
of untanned skin, and his equipments were completed by a small black hair cap set jauntily on
his head. He seemed satisfied with the result of
his examination, and said half aloud as he arose:
" Huron canoe — Huron moccasin — no Mohawk
thief — and now Pierre for Mons. le sauvage."
   Pierre had emigrated from France many years

before, and with the aid of his son had made himself useful as a hunter to the smaller outposts of the French. He supplied them with game. In one of their excursions the Mohawks came upon them, and after a long chase succeeded in killing and scalping the young man. Henceforth Pierre considered the Mohawks as his deadliest enemies. He had served as a spy under the great Champlain—a man dreaded by the Indians of every tribe, and whose name had become a war-cry to the French. Pierre was an expert woods-man, and an indefatigable Indian fighter—well known and loved by the Hurons, who gave him the sobriquet of *"L'Espion hardi."*

The Frenchman laughed as he entered the forest to meet the Indian. "Ho, ho, Huron," he shouted as he strode carelessly along. Watook heard the voice, and springing to a tree, cast his rifle into rest; but the dress and language of the speaker told him it was a friend, and he came leaping towards him.

"Ugh! L'Espion hardi! The pale-face is the friend of the Huron," he said.

"Very true, savage, very true."

"Has the Frenchman found any Hurons here?" and he waved his hand around.

"None but yourself, Huron."

Then Watook told him of the sad misfortune which had befallen his party, and of the capture of the two Frenchmen, and how he had come thither to gather the scattered Hurons and attempt a rescue. Exclamations of anger escaped the hunter as he listened to the story, and his manner became more grave.

"The scalp of the son of the Daring Scout hangs in the Mohawk lodge. Is his knife rusty; will he strike the trail of the Iroquois?" said the Indian in conclusion.

Pierre drew the weapon from his belt and ran his finger across its glittering blade—and his feeling deepened into fury as he remembered the sad day on which his son had perished.

"Huron," he said at length in a stern voice, "Huron! 'Daring Scout' will strike the Mohawk in his village;" then, recovering his wonted equanimity, continued:

"The braves probably went deep into the forest before they struck off towards the rendez-

vous—they will be here yet—for the current of
the river assisted you forward ahead of them; it
is rapid now. Let us build a fire and pass the
night here. No Mohawks are outlying now; for
the party you fell in with must have been a
strong one, and it is not likely that there is
another out. When the Hurons come in, we
will strike off through the forest to the trail of
your chief."

The counsel seemed wise to the Indian, and
they prepared to bivouac upon the spot. About
midnight the sound of a footstep struck upon the
ear of the Frenchman, who kept watch, sitting
at the foot of a tree shaded from the light of the
fire.

"Qui vive," said the hunter, who still adhered
somewhat to his old military habits: "Qui vive;"
but the figure approached, and the next moment
a Huron stalked up to the fire. Watook awoke
and greeted his comrade.

"The Hurons are scattered, and will come in
slowly, for they are very weary," said the stranger.
He made no other allusion to their late defeat.

When morning dawned, four or five warriors
8 *

had collected, and the impatient Watook proposed
to set out.

"No," said the Huron who had first come in;
"more braves come—more braves."

"They are already two days' march before
us," said Watook; but Pierre coincided with the
first. By the hour of noon about fifteen warriors
had assembled, some of them wounded, and all
wearied. Compelled by stern necessity, that
night they passed at the place of rendezvous, and
on the following morn set out, through the forest,
to strike on the trail of the Iroquois. . . . .

Night and morn came and went, night and
morn the captors and their captives toiled on
through the pathless forest. Still on—on went
the weary march; still on the rear of the con-
quering Mohawks hovered three dusky forms—
stern, silent, watchful.

CHAPTER VII.

THE RETURN.

ORNING Flower, why art thou sad? the young eagle of his tribe will soon return. Kiskepila will bring back the scalps of Huron warriors at his girdle: he will come back adorned with eagle-feathers, and the women of his tribe will sing his deeds. He will bring home many spoils, and will take the budding Flower of morn to bloom in his own lodge!"

"No, Dancing Fawn, the warriors of the tribe have been gone many days on the war-path. Many suns have set since the appointed hour of return passed by. The voices of the night have whispered in the ear of Morning Flower. Misfortune is on the path of the braves. He will return no more."

"Drooping Flower," said the other, drawing

up haughtily, " is not the blood of the conquer-
ing Iroquois in thy veins? and yet thou trem-
blest because the braves of the tribe outlie upon
the war-path a few suns longer than the appointed
time.   Thinkest thou that the Huron dogs could
withstand the invincible Mohawk? The Hurons
are cowards: they have forsaken Owaneeyo * for
the God of the pale-face, and Owaneeyo has
chilled their hearts and turned their blood to
water.   The Hurons are dogs!" and the speaker
tossed her hand contemptuously towards the
Huron country.

   She was a noble-looking Indian girl.   Her
black eye sparkled as she spoke, and the height-
ened color of her cheek betrayed the quick passion
of the untrained child of nature.   The other was
of gentle mood; her full and liquid eye looked
out softly from beneath the long and sweeping
lash that shaded its light.   Her hair was jetty
black, and, though straight, was finer and softer
than usual in the Indian race: it was braided in
glossy folds around her temples, and gathered in
a loop behind, bound up with bands of bright-

   * The owner and ruler of all things.

colored bark interwoven with beads. Her dress was a mantle, curiously wrought with gayly-colored feathers, and trimmed with tufts of elk-hair dyed red, thrown gracefully around her form, leaving her left arm and shoulder bare. Her limbs were finely moulded.

Below the maidens stretched a scene of great beauty. From two hills, covered with heavy forest-trees, an open sward sloped gradually on either side, until both blended into a little plain between traversed by a small stream, on whose banks a group of children were playing busily — now plunging into the shallow waters, and now sunning themselves upon the soft and luxuriant grass that bordered it. On the northern side, where the descent faced full towards the south, was ranged a number of Indian wigwams, in the centre of which stood the council-lodge, rising conspicuous above the rest of the village. Before the doors of some of the cabins groups of old men and children were gathered, while the squaws were passing to and fro, engaged in their domestic labors. At the edge of the forest a number of youths were practising with the bow and arrow.

The western portion of the slope was filled with young corn, green and luxuriant in its growth, with its white tassels and ears already blooming out. On the southern bank of the stream swept upwards a gentle ascent of beautiful green-sward, gayly interspersed with the gloriously tinted wild flowers that adorn the fields of America. Around this little valley, like a palisade, stood the edge of the forest, its interminable depths stretching far away towards the horizon, until, like the green waters of a vast ocean, its waving foliage seemed to mingle with the distant sky.

The two Indian maidens reclined upon the soft turf at the edge of the forest above the village, and for a few moments gazed down in silence upon the valley. The thick foliage of a massive oak overhung them, and shaded them from the warm rays of the sun.

"Dancing Fawn," at length resumed the young girl, "the French warriors are terrible in battle, riding fierce horses, and with their breasts clad in steel; perchance the braves have fallen in with them and been cut off."

"False Mohawk girl, have not the braves of

our nation met the French in battle? Their
war-cry is like the roar of Unghiara * — the
Huron and the pale-faces tremble at its sound.
But listen, Morning Flower! heard you that
faint shout? See! it has aroused the village!"

The young maidens arose from their recumbent position, and awaited in expectation the
event. The village below them now exhibited
a different and more lively aspect. The youths
had quitted their pastime and gathered around
the council-lodge where the old men of the tribe
had assembled. The women had left their occu-
pations, and were clamorously joining the group.
At length another yell broke from the forest far
to the east, and came faintly swelling to the
expectant crowd. In a few moments more a
runner emerged from the forest, and, loping
down the hill, hurried on towards the village.
As he approached, the assemblage opened to
receive him, and he paused in silence before the
chief, who was surrounded by a group of vener-
able warriors. Kiodego † motioned him to speak.

* Niagara.
† "A settler of disputes."

"The braves of the Mohawks," said the runner, "are mighty warriors; their arms are strong, and the Hurons' are dogs. The French become women before the battle-axes of the Mohawks. The warriors bring back scalps and many prisoners; they have captured the great medicine of the French; they have routed and slain many Hurons." Then he recounted the names of the wounded — for of the dead the Indian speaks not. As he mentioned the name of Kiskepila, the son of the old chief, a deep sigh broke from the lips of the Morning Flower, and her head sunk for a moment upon her breast. Then she raised it up proudly, and fierce determination lit up her beautiful features. Gloom had passed away. Kiodego sat unmoved, evincing no concern for the misfortune of his son. As the runner finished his recital, a shout broke from the assemblage, which was answered from the forest by a succession of yells, whose increasing tone marked the near approach of the conquerors; it was the scalp-whoop. Then came another succession of yells, one for each prisoner. At this signal the crowd around the council-

lodge dispersed to the different wigwams, but
soon reassembled, every one armed with weapons
of some kind; knives, tomahawks, stones, and
war-clubs. As soon as the runner appeared,
Morning Flower and her companion had descended and mingled with the group before the
lodge, and now, armed like the other women of
the tribe, they hurried off towards the edge of
the forest. It would have been difficult to
recognize the sorrowing, lone, lorn Indian
maiden with the drooping glance, in the excited
form that wound amid the group, urging on her
sister furies to greater frenzy.

"The Gentle Flower," she said to Dancing
Fawn, "is a Mohawk maiden; a thorn has
pierced through her moccasin and wounded her
foot. She will pluck it out, and with it tear the
flesh of the Frenchman. The Morning Flower
will avenge the wound of Kiskepila!" ·

The inhabitants of the village had arranged
themselves in two lines on the open space south
of the little rivulet, for by that side the war-
party, having made a detour in the forest, were
to enter on the valley. Thus the lines ran from

9   G

the south-west up towards the village. Old
women with staves, young gentle maidens with
heavy clubs, youths with knives and tomahawks,
and even the little naked children, with sharp
stones, stood waiting, with savage exultation, for
the coming of the prisoners.

The triumphant songs of the returning warriors
became every moment more distinct; at length,
far down the shaded avenues of the forest, the
front of the body appeared in view. A cry of
wild joy broke from the expectant savages, and
the two lines waved and undulated along their
whole length, as each person endeavored to catch
a glimpse of the triumphant braves. On they
came!—the warrior stepping more firmly, and
erecting his head more proudly, as he beheld the
old men of his village at the council-lodge, in the
distance, and, nearer, the women and the children
who would sing his gallant deeds, and the youths
who would learn to emulate his fame. On they
came, swinging high the scalps they had taken,
the bloody trophies of their victory, and chant-
ing the story of their actions. At length they
emerged from the forest, and stood in the bright

sun upon the beautiful green slope of verdure.
The prisoners were grouped together; their
captors now singled them out, preparing them
to start upon the fearful trial which awaited
them. Father Laval was pale and jaded; his
face was scarred and bruised, and the clotted
blood still disfigured his wounded features; his
hands were yet bound behind him. A Mohawk
approached to sever the cord; the flesh had so
swollen around the tight band as almost to conceal it, and the knife of the savage gashed the
hands of the priest. Released from their con-
finement, his arms fell heavily to his side,
inanimate, and refusing to obey the stiff and
swollen muscles. The blood began to creep
slowly in the veins, and the sensation of numb-
ness was succeeded by one of acute pain. The
Indian then loosed the band which confined the
black robe of the Jesuit around his body. His
outer garment was next taken off, and Father
Laval stood half unrobed; his shirt was stained
with blood, and his naked feet and legs were
torn and bleeding, and festering with thorns
and briers; every step left its mark in blood.

The work of the Indian was soon done, and
the captives were prepared to run the gauntlet.
The tender frame of the young novice, with the
red blood incrusted upon his delicate skin, and
his limbs bruised and swollen, and almost helpless, contrasted strangely with the massive pro-
portions of Le Loup, who still kept close beside
him, ready to aid him in his need. Strong, and
seemingly unwearied, the Huron stood up like a
mighty statue of bronze, heedless of the many
wounds upon his limbs and breast. "My
father!" he said to the Jesuit, as they neared
each other for a moment, "my father, when Le
Loup springs forward between the lines, hasten
on, and seek to avoid the blows of the Iroquois!
Make for the war-post by the council-lodge —
gain it, and you are safe!"

Rene Bourdoise turned towards the spot indicated by Le Loup to the Jesuit, and his heart
shrunk within him. A hundred yelling furies,
with clubs and knives, were between them and
the place of refuge, and his limbs were faint and
weary. He raised his soul to God.

"Fear not, brother," said Le Loup, "but
gather up all thy strength."

"I will trust in God," replied the novice, sadly.

"It is the eve of the Assumption of the Blessed Virgin, my son," exclaimed the Jesuit. "Let us place ourselves under her special protection. She will intercede for our safety; or if it be God's holy will, she will obtain for us strength to win the crown of Martyrdom. And lo!" he added, his countenance gleaming with joy, and his worn and weakened form swelling erect with enthusiasm, "and lo! the blood of our Martyrdom, of our triumph on the eve of her glorious and triumphant Assumption into Heaven, may become the forerunner of her Patronage over this new land. With our sufferings, however unworthy, let us dedicate it to her invocation!"

At length the word was given: "Joggo!"— "go!"—and the prisoners started. The powerful Huron broke away at a swinging trot, which puzzled Father Laval to equal. Le Loup made for the opening of the lines: a hundred arms were uplifted to strike—knives glistened, and the whole gang of furies yelled with a savage delight. The strong runner paused for a moment till the

9 *

Jesuit was close behind him, then bounding forward, he dashed fiercely into the midst of the
crowd, casting aside their blows and overturning
many in his path. Yet he did not pass scatheless,
and, ere he had gone half the distance, the blood
was streaming from his wounded body. The
whole rage of the whippers was in a moment
turned upon him, for he had succeeded in baffling
many of them, and they were pursuing him regardless of the rest, and permitting the two
Frenchmen to escape with little suffering. But
there was one whose passion was not to be led off.
Morning Flower scorned to wreak her vengeance
upon the Huron, for she conceived that none but
the Frenchman could have stricken down the
Young Eagle. Her eye was turned upon the
Jesuit, whom she saw passing almost unharmed
in the rear of the powerful warriors. At length
Father Laval came near her, hastening forward
at as great speed as his swollen and stiffened
limbs would permit. She grasped a club of hard-
ened wood in her hand—her arm was raised—the
Jesuit cast an imploring look upon her, but the
heart of the girl was steeled to pity; her savage

nature was unyielding, and she struck him a
heavy blow. He staggered forward, about to
fall; at the next moment he was raised and
hurried forward by the arm of one of his Huron
neophytes. Blinded and stunned by the shower
of blows which fell upon him, he still pressed
forward, awaiting every moment the final stroke,
which would close his sufferings, when suddenly
it seemed to him that a new vigor was infused
into his limbs, that he walked erect and unfalter-
ingly among his raging persecutors, while amid a
radiance enclosing him as within a veil of glory,
broke upon his astonished eyes a vision of celes-
tial beauty whose pitying eye, and glowing heart
and outstretched helping hands, consoled, encour-
aged, guided and protected him. At length he
knelt safe from further harm at the war-post, and
ere he arose from his prayer of gratitude, the beauteous vision had faded from his eyes — though its
impress never left his heart. A wild spectacle
met his eye as he gazed over the field through
which he had just passed. The tall Huron, Le
Loup, heedless of blows and wounds, was still
struggling through the savage throng, carrying

the main body of the whippers after him and
around him. Ever as he turned and doubled, a
portion of his tormentors would start before him
to cut off his escape; then, like the hunted wolf,
he would burst upon them with all his strength,
and break through them — only to find another
body ready to receive him. A group of old
squaws, armed like fiends with the worst weapons
they could obtain, pointed and jagged stones,
sharpened sticks and knives, attempted to stop
his course. He dashed into the midst of them,
striking the first to the earth before she could aim
a blow; yelling horribly as she fell, she clasped
the warrior's feet and tripped him up. With his
outstretched arms he grasped several of his persecutors, and they came to the ground together:
his pursuers, close at his heels, fell over them,
and the living pile struggled together in inextri-
cable confusion, striking and beating each other
indiscriminately. A shout of laughter broke
from the Mohawk warriors, who watched the
scene with interest. Winding out from the living
mass that was piled up above him, the Huron
sprang again to his feet and started off, delivered

from more than half his pursuers, who still lay struggling together—the upper ones believing that their victim was still in their power, while the efforts made by those underneath to arise made the confusion still more dire. The Huron was speeding on.

Half-way to the post tottered on the poor novice, Rene Bourdoise, his young limbs stiff and fainting. Ah! little did he think, when he quitted the shores of beautiful and gentle France, of the wild scenes of suffering and torture he was to endure for the sake of Christ in the dreary wilderness of the west. The companions of his early days were wandering through the bright valleys of his native land; songs of joy were upon their lips, glad music ringing in their ears, loving hearts and tender hands around them. In his ear rang the yell of the wild Mohawk, and the hand of the pitiless savage was upon him. Then he called to mind his solemn vocation, and devoting himself to suffering, clasped his hands towards heaven, and struggled on.

"Grant me strength to bear my cross, O God!" he said.

The novice had already reached the stream:
he had received little else but passing blows, for
the strong Hurons afforded better game to these
human hunters.   The younger and the weaker,
who feared to grapple with the stout warriors,
alone pursued him.   But now a party rushed
towards him, and in an instant the fainting youth
sunk beneath their blows.   It was at the moment
that Le Loup approached the creek.   His eye
rested upon the novice as he fell among his tormentors, and he dashed through their midst drawing them after him in the race.   Rene Bourdoise
arose—the Indians were already in another portion of the field, and he passed the stream, and,
painfully toiling up the hill, touched the war-
post.   At length the chase began to flag, and Le
Loup, having succeeded in doubling on his pursuers, leaped up the hill to the goal.   The last
Huron soon came in.

The overthrown squaws, bruised and beaten,
gathered round the group of captives, and with
loud imprecations menaced the cause of their
misfortunes with the vengeance of the tribe.

"Ah!" said one, "wait, when the Huron is

bound to the post and the flames are kindled around him, we will torture the dog till he screams with pain."

"Yes, the Mohawk women will make the Huron warrior yell with the torment," and the fiends shouted in anticipation of the sacrifice. Le Loup looked calmly on and smiled.

The prisoners were again bound, and, the ceremonies attendant upon the return of the war-party having been gone through, were placed under a guard in the council-lodge, while the warriors dispersed through the village, each with his band of friends and admirers. A portion of the war-party belonged to another village; these were entertained with dances and feasting until towards evening, when they took their departure for their own homes, contrary to their usual custom, leaving the prisoners at the first village to be disposed of by a joint council at some future day.

CHAPTER VIII.

BAPTISM IN BONDAGE.

THE forest to the north of the village was filled with undergrowth, and was wild and rocky, rising at times into hills of considerable size, which swept gradually down until they melted in the gentle ascent upon which the Mohawk village stood. Towards the close of the day which had been signalized by the return of the war-party, a solitary Indian cautiously made his way through the thick bushes, replacing every leaf and branch in its position, and covering each footstep as he passed. His course was turned in the direction of the wildest of the hills. As he proceeded, the ground became more broken and rocky until a huge ledge rose abruptly in the forest, jutting almost over the summits of the oaks. At the foot of the cliff he paused for a

moment, and surveyed the face and summit of
the rock. He seemed satisfied, and moved along
the base of the ledge until he reached a part that
was less precipitous, and was covered with bushes
and creepers growing out of the many crevices
and spots of earth upon its sides. Here he
paused for a moment, and, having made a low
signal, which was answered from above, began to
ascend. A little distance from the summit, the
rock receded until it opened into something like
a cave, which was completely hidden from below
by the bushes and wild vines in bloom, which
here clustered thick upon the side of the ascent.
At the farther end of the recess sat two figures,
silent and motionless; their rifles * were lying
near them. The Indian entered and took his
seat by his companions; at length he spoke,
pointing with his hand over his shoulder towards
the village.

"The Hurons and the blackgown are in the

* This term has been used throughout this story; perhaps *musket* would have been more correct, though at the
date of the story few Indians were possessed of fire-arms at
all. The Mohawks obtained them at an earlier period,
having been supplied by the Dutch traders.

10

council-lodge. No more gauntlet; the warriors from the other villages have gone," he said, and held up the fingers of both hands twice to indicate their number. "So many braves at the village," and he again held up his fingers till they indicated forty; "must wait." The Hurons assented, and Ahasistari continued: "The black-gown is weak and bruised; many days must pass before he can travel again to the river. The Hurons must tarry till they can go as fast as the Mohawk, or the foe will gather from the tribes and follow on the trail."

At length one of the Hurons spoke: "Watook may collect the braves, and be here in another sun."

"Quickfoot," said Ahasistari, "it is better that he should lie out with the warriors some distance in the forest. There is a little stream a day's journey from the village of the Mohawks; we crossed it on the trail. Let him hide upon its banks. If he come nearer, a wandering Mohawk might strike upon his trail, and then all hope will be lost. We cannot attempt a rescue until the blackgowns are strong enough to journey

with us. Watook and his braves will follow the
trail of the Mohawks; Quickfoot must retrace it,
and meet him. He will bid him to remain until
Ahasistari commands again."

"Good," said the Huron, and, taking up his
rifle, wearied as he was, with the elastic tread of
the brave, departed. The others sat still.

Ahasistari and his two followers had hovered
around the trail of the Mohawks, but as the foe
was very numerous—about fifty warriors in all—
had not obtained a single opportunity of attempt-
ing the rescue of the prisoners by artifice; of
course force was out of the question. It now
became necessary for the chief to delay his opera-
tions for the reasons which he gave his followers,
and also in the hope that the number of the warriors at the village might be reduced by some
new expedition, and thus afford a favorable
opportunity of making an assault, with whatever braves Watook might bring up, to whom
he could at any time transmit his orders by his
remaining companion. In the meantime, too,
some chance of a successful stratagem might present itself, and he determined to watch the vil-

lage closely to secure if possible the escape of his friends.

When the Mohawks had approached the end of their journey, the Hurons forsook their trail, and struck off through the forest to the hills, among which they were now concealed, having perceived them on their path from the summit of a distant elevation. The track of a fox led them up the ledge of rocks to the cave, and at the same time gave them the assurance that it was altogether unfrequented by their foes. Leaving his companions, Ahasistari then crept stealthily towards the village, and reached it in time to be a witness from a neighboring thicket of all the scenes which followed upon the arrival of the war-party, and learned from a single glance the condition of the captives. His plans were formed, and he returned to the rocks to carry them out. With twenty good braves he would not have hesitated to attack the village, knowing the vast advantage which darkness and surprise give to even a few assailants over a larger number, mingled with women and children, and unprepared for battle. The village, too, was not de-

fended by any stockade or fortification, for such
was the terror of the Mohawk name that few of
their enemies dared to set foot upon their territory.
But Ahasistari deemed it more prudent to post-
pone the attempt, judging, from the departure of
the braves of the neighboring village without
carrying with them a portion of the prisoners,
that for the present they were in no danger of
public execution. Such, however, he knew to
be the passionate cruelty of the Iroquois that any
one of them might be sacrificed at a moment.
This danger could not be avoided.

The night that followed was a festive one in
the village of the Mohawks. Long continued
were the rejoicings of the people over the valor
of the braves, and it was determined in council
to dispatch runners to Fort Orange with a portion
of the booty, which had been large, to procure
" fire-water " from the traders for a solemn festival over the victory. In the midst of all this
joy, many sleepless hours had passed over the
heads of the two Frenchmen. Sore, bruised,
suffering intense pain, unable to lie at ease, slumber long delayed to shroud their weariness in

10*   H

oblivion. At length it came. The Hurons, after the prayers of the night had been said, soon yielded to sleep, accustomed as they were to catch repose in any attitude. Day broke gayly over the village, and the rays of the bright sun stole in through the chinks of the council-lodge, and rested in golden streaks upon the hard-trodden earthen floor. As the luminary rose higher in the sky, a beam, playing through a narrow crevice, crept slowly over the pale face of the young novice. His lips were drawn apart, a fixed expression of pain dwelt upon his features, and his heavy and disturbed breathing denoted the fever that raged in his veins. He slept on; the joyous ray playing upon his sad features, myriads of motes holding their gay revels in its beams. Near him slumbered Father Laval. The Hurons were stretched around upon the floor in deep sleep. At the door of the lodge sat the guard, his head resting upon his knee, and his quick eye occasionally scanning the slumberers; but for its motion he would have seemed as rapt in sleep as they. Time passed on; the sounds without told that the village was again all alive,

and one by one the Hurons awoke from their
long repose, and, stretching their cramped limbs
as best they might, arose to a sitting posture.
A single glance of his eye was all the notice the
guard deigned to bestow upon their movements.
The two Frenchmen still slept on. At length
Father Laval awoke. For a moment he gazed
around unable to realize his situation; then turning himself, he endeavored to kneel; the effort
was painful, but he succeeded. Rene Bourdoise
now opened his eyes, but he was unable to move.

" Do not seek to rise, my son," said the Jesuit,
"you are too weak; the prayer of the heart is
acceptable to God, whether you kneel or not."
Then Father Laval addressed the Hurons : " My
children, from the midst of our sufferings let us
cry out to heaven for mercy, not for the bodies
which are of earth and perishable, but for the
souls which are immortal, undying. Let us be-
seech our heavenly Father to accept our sufferings
here in atonement through the blood of his Son
for the sins of our past lives. Let us not repine.
We suffer—'it is for the greater glory of God.'
He will draw good for us out of this evil. Let

us pray; let us join in spirit with our brethren
of the mission of St. Mary in the holy sacrifice
of the altar."

The Indians listened in silence, and the Jesuit
prayed aloud.   Many moments passed thus in
holy prayer and meditation. Streams of heavenly
consolation seemed to pour down upon the priest
and his little flock.   Rapt in holy abstraction,
their sufferings were all forgotten; and, seated in
heart at the foot of the Saviour's cross, their own
sorrows dwindled into nothingness in the contemplation of his infinite passion.   Then the stern
spirit of the Hurons melted, and the enduring
warrior became the contrite penitent.

"The anger of the Iroquois is unsparing, my
father.   Death may be ours at any moment,"
said Le Loup, as the consoling prayer was ended.

"True, my son; let us prepare to meet it;"
and the Indian, moving nearer to the priest, began
his confession.   It was done; and the Jesuit pronounced the words of absolution in virtue of that
power committed by Christ to his church, "Whose
sins ye shall forgive, they are forgiven."

"Go in peace!" said the priest, and another

and another came. Often before had these Christian savages, in their unsophisticated nature, made public confession of their faults, seeking to humble themselves before heaven and earth, and thus to show the sincerity of their repentance and to do penance by mortifying their pride and self-love : now therefore they did not heed the presence of their brethren. Two there were who were yet unbaptized, two neophytes longing for the redeeming waters of the purifying sacrament. In turn they knelt and confessed themselves, and besought baptism. Alas! the good priest, bound hand and foot, without a drop of water, was unable to administer the sacred rite.

The pious occupation of the prisoners was at length interrupted by the entrance of a warrior, who was soon followed by another. It was not long before a number had gathered in the lodge. One of the Mohawks, at length, approached the Jesuit, and loosed the cords that bound him ; then he released the young novice. Father Laval sat still for some moments, endeavoring to overcome the stiffness of his limbs. Whilst he remained in this position, an Indian entered the lodge, bearing

in his hand an ear of corn upon the stock, which
he had just plucked; he threw it to the Jesuit.
The sunlight played upon it as it lay—and see!
upon its silken beard and broad blade clung little
drops of dew *—sparkling and glistening, like
jewels in the light! Ah! far more precious at that
moment than all the diamonds of Golconda!—
There was enough to baptize the two captive
Hurons. Taking it up carefully, he arose, zeal
and joy overcoming pain and weakness, and
knelt above the prostrate neophytes.

"O my children, the hand of the ever merciful
is with us. Kneel—kneel!" and in the wild forest
lodge, made holy as God's temple by the prayers
and sufferings of his faithful children, with the
Christian Huron and wild Mohawk looking on,
without sponsor, with no lights but God's own
sunlight, with no incense but the ineffably sweet
incense of humble prayer, before the altar of the
heart, the priest admitted the rejoicing neophytes
into the fold of Christ, into the household of

* This incident is related of Father Isaac Jones, while a
captive among the Mohawks, by Bancroft, almost in the
words used above. See *Bancroft*, vol. iii. p. 138.

faith, sprinkling the pure dew of heaven upon their uplifted brows. Wondrously solemn was that simple baptism in the wilderness; in the midst of trials and sufferings, in the face of death. No swelling organ arose over the sacrament; no swinging bell pealed out; no white robe upon the neophyte, but the stainless one of purity of heart; no vestment on the priest but the martyr's, stained with blood.

"Come sorrow; come death," exclaimed the Jesuit; "I will heed them not, O God! for of thy mercy there is no end."

Scarcely had he finished before an Indian summoned him to follow him. Father Laval left the lodge. A group of boys were gathered before the door, and watched the priest with interest as he passed through them, but did not molest him. His conductor, crossing the open space around the lodge, turned his steps towards a tent at the end of the village near the forest. This rude dwelling of the savage was constructed of poles sunk in the ground, in a circle, with their tops bent to a common point and fastened together. Over this frame was stretched a canopy of buffalo skins,

stitched together with thread made of the tendons
of the deer. It was large and commodious, and
betokened the wealth and standing of its owner.
In front, the two ends of the covering hung apart,
leaving a space for entrance, which was usually
closed up by a single buffalo robe suspended from
a cross piece above. This was, of course, raised
to admit light and air. The tent was of far better order than the lodges around it, which were
rude huts covered with bark. The Indian motioned Father Laval to enter. Lying on a couch
of skins, the Jesuit beheld the young chief whose
wounds he had bound up on the field of battle.
An old man sat near him; it was the father of
Kiskepila, and the chief of the village. The priest
approached the couch of the wounded man to
feel his pulse, but the old man waved him away
with a motion of his hand.

"Pale-face!" he said in the Huron tongue,
"you are the foe of the Mohawks, and yet you
sought to heal the wounds of Kiskepila."

"I am the foe of no people," replied the Jesuit,
meekly; "my mission is to save, not to destroy."

"Thou art the friend of the Huron?" said the
old man interrogatively.

"Dost thou see the sun?" said the priest. "The God who created it made it to shine alike upon the Huron and the Mohawk. Its beams ripen the corn in the country of the Iroquois, and in the lands beyond the great lakes. Will the Mohawk veil his eyes to the sunlight because its rays shine upon the Huron too?" The Indian was silent, and the Jesuit continued:

"The Great Spirit loves all his children, the Mohawk and the Huron; will the wise and brave Mohawk shut his ears to the words of the Great Spirit because the. Huron has already heard them?"

"Pale-face, the Mohawk listens to the voice of Owaneeyo; he hears it in the forest, and in the waters, and in the winds!"

"The Great Spirit has taught us, sachem, to love those who hate us — to love all men — to let our hearts shine on all like the sun of heaven!"

"*Hugh!*" exclaimed the Mohawk, "does the pale-face speak with a forked tongue? The Iroquois *strikes* his enemy, and it is *good!*" and he laid his hand upon his heart.

Father Laval paused for a moment ere he

11

answered this appeal to the natural passions of
man as an argument against the truth of the
Christian doctrine, and then, pointing to the
wounded man, said : "Kiskepila sought the life
of the pale-face — "

"And the pale-face saved the life of Kiskepila,"
interrupted the young brave in a tone of deep
feeling. "The words of the blackgown are true.
The wolf kills the deer, the bear the buffalo, the
hawk the dove, and the Mohawk his wounded
foe. It is only the pale-face—the blackgown —
that binds up the wounds of his enemy. His
heart is gentle as the summer breeze!"

Silence ensued, for the Indian scarcely knew
how to receive and estimate the wonderful mag-
nanimity of Christianity. Nature taught him
to do good for good ; to return good for evil was
a new thought to him, yet it awoke a slumbering
chord of the heart ; he began to feel the sublim-
ity of the precept, and was silent. At this point
of the conversation a squaw entered the lodge,
bearing several ears of young corn, and a quan-
tity of beans which had been roasted at a fire
without, and placed them on a mat upon the
floor.

"Eat!" said the chief. Father Laval approached, and making the sign of the cross, blessed the simple provisions which had been offered to him, and then proceeded to satisfy his famished appetite. Hitherto he had been furnished with barely enough food to support his strength, for it was a common mode of torture among the Indians to make their prisoners pass days and nights together with barely enough food to sustain life, and yet inflict an incredible amount of suffering. Yet he ate moderately. A gourd of water was placed beside him — he had not slaked his thirst for many hours — it was grateful to his burning lips. Having returned thanks to God, he arose and approached the couch. The chief again spoke: "The pale-face made a sign upon his forehead?"

"It was the sign of the cross," replied the Jesuit.

The chief nodded his head affirmatively. "I thank the Great Spirit for his gifts."

Then the Jesuit began to examine the wounds of Kiskepila, and to bind them anew, all the while explaining the meaning of the holy sym-

bol which he had used; how God had sent his
Son on earth after the sin of our first parents,
and how his chosen people had scourged and put
him to death upon the cross, and how, ever since
then, his followers had used that sign to recall to
their minds the recollection of his agony and
death.

"Ugh! Dogs!" exclaimed Kiskepila, as he
shook his clenched fist. The old chief listened
with a look of incredulity.

While the priest was speaking, a figure glided
softly in at the opening of the tent, and crouched
silently in an obscure corner with the females of
the family. Morning Flower listened: she could
understand but little, for he spoke in the Huron
dialect. In astonishment, she gazed upon him
as he tenderly bound up the wounds of her
lover. The passion of the previous evening had
subsided, and she remembered with a sorrowing
heart that she had tortured him in the gauntlet.
Hers was a gentle spirit in spite of its wild edu-
cation. She arose, approached the priest, and
looked him in the face; at the same moment the
young warrior, pointing to the Jesuit, said:

"Morning Flower, the blackrobe saved the life of Kiskepila when the Young Eagle had slain his people — the Hurons."

Then the heart of the woman was true, and, in spite of early habits and barbarous training, beat there as nature made it. A gush of remorse filled her soul, and with a low wild cry she broke away from the tent. The two Mohawks looked at each other in astonishment, unable to comprehend the cause of so singular an exhibition of feeling; and the elder exclaimed in low tone, "Hugh! Medicine!" and shook his head, attributing the action of the girl to some species of enchantment on the part of the priest. But Father Laval well understood it: he recognized the maiden who had so relentlessly pursued him whilst running the gauntlet: yet he continued the conversation, without heeding the circumstance further.

At length the Jesuit returned to the council-lodge, where he busied himself in ministering to the wounded Hurons. Rene Bourdoise, released from the tight bonds which had been so painful, began to recover a little from the weakness that

11 *

had rendered him helpless. With a tottering step he descended to the stream, and washed the blood from his face and hands, and laved his swollen feet. The cool water refreshed and strengthened him, calming the fever of his veins. He found a gourd upon the bank, and filling it, bore it to the famished prisoners at the lodge. The Jesuit assisted the novice, unheeded by the Mohawks, who listlessly reclined on the grass, occasionally casting a glance upon the prisoners, to see that no attempt was made to loosen their bonds.

Towards evening the Jesuit again entered the tent of Kiodego. Kiskepila was resting in a half recumbent position, supported by a pile of furs that a king might have envied. Many days had passed since his wounds had been received, for the march was long and tedious, and he was now recruiting his strength. Father Laval again felt his pulse, for he feared lest the fatigue of a long journey, upon a rough litter, might bring on a fever which would prove fatal; but a skilful preparation of draughts from herbs and roots had prevented it: the stroke was still calm and regular. Then he entered into conversation with the young brave, using, as much as possible, the Mohawk tongue, earnestly seeking to become familiar with it for "the greater glory of God." In the tedious and painful route he had caught a knowledge of it from his captors, and its affinity with the Huron tongue, which he spoke with ease and fluency, enabled him to make rapid progress. The young warrior listened to him patiently, but as soon as he paused, addressed him:

"Blackgown, you have taught me that the pale-face loves all, and forgives those who have injured him. Morning Flower," — and the young maiden, springing up from a group of females in the farther part of the tent, approached and stood beside the priest, — "Morning Flower, when the blood of Kiskepila was flowing from his veins, and his heart was growing cold, the hand of the pale-face stopped its flow. Blackgown, Morning Flower is the destined bride of Kiskepila."

The priest placed his hands upon the head of the young girl, and then, raising them up to heaven, uttered a prayer for the wild but gentle spirit before him. "O God, grant that the light of thy faith may pierce the heart of this untutored girl, and of all here. Mary, mother of the sorrowful, bring these wanderers to the faith of thy Son by the powerful intercession of thy prayers." And he added, in the Mohawk tongue, "Daughter, peace be with thee."

Then Father Laval began to discourse again upon the subject of his morning's conversation, speaking in the Mohawk dialect as well as he could. Kiskepila listened attentively, and the maiden, seated at her lover's feet, gathered every word that fell from the lips of the priest.

When the Jesuit had departed, the young warrior conversed with Morning Flower upon the discourse which they had heard, explaining such portions as had been uttered in the Huron dialect, and wondering over that which was mysterious and difficult, for it is hard to express abstract ideas in the Indian language. The kindness and attention of the missionary had won the heart of the young Iroquois, and, finding that he acted out in his own life what he taught to others, under the impulse of a grateful feeling, he lent a willing ear to his words. Kiskepila had a clear head, and the very fact that the Jesuit faced so many dangers, and endured so much toil and suffering, to preach the doctrines of his religion, satisfied him at once of the uprightness and sincerity of his motives. The skill and knowledge of the Frenchman proved to him that he was no ordinary man, and he inclined to believe even the wonderful tidings he announced. Yet doubts met him at every point as he thought over the strange things he had been told. When, therefore, the Jesuit entered the tent on the following day, he questioned him:

"Blackgown, you tell me that the Saviour died and was buried, and that on the third day he arose again from the dead. I have never seen the dead arise—how can I believe it?"

"My son, it would have been no proof of his divinity if rising from the dead had been an ordinary occurrence. But he is God. He it was who made the law that all men should die, and that law he could suspend or alter. As man he died; as God-man he arose. The people of thy

I

tribe believe that the spirits of the departed do
not die; can not the God who preserves the spirit
preserve also the body, and give it back to life?
Can he not at a word bid the tomb to open, and
the lifeless corpse to live and breathe again? Ah,
my son! there are no laws to bind the Omnipo-
tent God but the laws of his own mercy and
justice and eternal providence. He has been
pleased to listen to the prayer of his humble
followers upon this earth, and has for them
wrought miracles almost equally wonderful.
The Blessed Xavier, on the shore of the far east,
knelt and prayed, and the ear of the Almighty
was inclined towards him, and when the holy
priest stretched forth his hand, and called upon
the dead to come forth from his silent grave, the
lifeless sprung up into strength and health and
beauty."

A deep exclamation of surprise broke from the
lips of the attentive Indian, whilst the women of
the family gathered nearer to hear the words of
the animated speaker. Warmed with a holy
zeal, the Jesuit continued in a clear firm
voice:

"The resurrection of the Saviour from the dead was to be the final seal of salvation; it was to open the way for us from the tomb to heaven!"

Then Father Laval went on to tell how, ages before his coming, the mode of his birth, his suffering, the miracles which he was to perform, his passion and his death had been foretold, and how exactly they had been accomplished; and he summed up all the evidences of Christianity, while the young warrior listened attentively, often bowing his head in token of assent.

"Yes, it must be true," he said at length, after the Jesuit had concluded: "Kiskepila must believe."

Thus Father Laval sought every opportunity to impress upon the mind of the young warrior the truths of Christianity, and the relation which existed between them made the young Iroquois listen with a docility unexampled among that fierce race. Whatever the young man learned he was sure to communicate to Morning Flower, who soon began to seek occasions of conversing with the priest, and listened with admiration to his accounts of the splendor of the cities of France,

and the number of their inhabitants, things like
the wonders of fairy tales to her unsophisticated
imagination. With these accounts the priest
always mingled descriptions of the splendid
churches and of the gorgeous ceremonial, of the
sacred rites performed within them, to the honor
and glory of God, and explained them to the
maiden as well as he could in his imperfect knowledge of the language.   Then, leaving these sub-
jects, he would converse upon the moral relations
of Christian society, instruct her in the duties of
woman, and teach her the obligations of religion,
the sanctity of marriage, and the beauty and
holiness of purity of heart and body.   Morning
Flower drank in his words, and kept them in her
heart.   But this was the work of days.   In the
meanwhile the village was filled with various
accounts of the conversations which the priest had
held in the tent of Kiodego — how he had spoken
of wonderful and mysterious things, and how he
had said that the fathers of the blackgown, in
times not long gone by, had called the dead from
their tombs.   These reports, increased and dis-
torted as they passed from mouth to mouth, cast

a species of awe around the priest in the eyes of many. He began to be looked upon as a magician or medicine more powerful than their own. Yet, unconscious of all this, the humble Jesuit pursued his labors with increasing assiduity.

12

CHAPTER IX.

THE COUNCIL.

EVERY night Father Laval and the novice had been bound and confined with the other prisoners in the lodge. In the meanwhile Rene Bourdoise began to gain strength, for Morning Flower, compassionating his sufferings, extended her kindness towards him, and supplied him, as well as Father Laval, with food, in addition to that distributed by their captors. A little gentle exercise, and hours of rest, assisted nature wonderfully in her recuperative efforts: but although the two Frenchmen recruited each day in health, they were still subject to all the petulant cruelty of the Iroquois. Still it was only that common torture which every captive was made to endure, and though great in itself, dwindled away into littleness when met by their boundless patience and tranquillity of heart.

A week had passed, but there seemed to be no disposition on the part of the Mohawk warriors to leave their village even upon a hunting expedition. It was the corn moon, and plenty surrounded them — and the Indian is always satisfied if the present moment be provided for. They were awaiting the return of the runners with the fire-water from Fort Orange. Towards the evening of the sixth day these messengers came back unexpectedly to the village, having met a Dutch trader some days' journey from the village, and purchased from him the necessary supply. It was now determined by the braves that a council should be held on the following day to decide upon the fate of the prisoners; and a portion of the fire-water was set aside for the carousings which would follow upon such a proceeding. A runner was therefore at once dispatched to the village which had joined in the war-party, inviting the presence of a deputation to assist at the council.

Father Laval, who had already retired to the

council-lodge, watched these proceedings with a troubled eye; he saw bustle and preparation, but was unable to conceive its object. Le Loup sat coldly watching the movements of the Iroquois, knowing too well what was likely to ensue. The Jesuit at length turned an inquiring eye upon him, and questioned him:

"What is the cause of all this commotion, my son?"

"*Fire-water!*" said Le Loup, sententiously. "The runners have come back from the traders, and the Mohawk will be crazy to-night — he will kill if he can."

"If he can? — alas! there is nothing to prevent him; then, my children, we must look upon death as immediately before us, and be ready to meet him like Christian men!"

"Good!" said Le Loup emphatically; "but they will not all drink — they will cast lots, who shall be guard — *may* kill, though. It is good to be ready!"

At length the council-lodge was closed up and fastened firmly, while it was evident to the prisoners that a double guard was placed over them, to protect them from any attempts which might be made against them by the intoxicated Indians in the fury of their orgies. The noise without began to increase, and soon became uproarious. The greater portion of the intoxicating liquid had been carefully concealed in order that it might be preserved for the second festival, in pursuance of the plan adopted. The intoxication therefore, of the braves, scarcely reached to that point of frenzy when the whole passion of the savage is aroused and nothing but blood will satisfy him. Yet now and then an Indian, more excited than the rest, would approach the lodge with reeling step, but flashing eye, and endeavor to force his way to the prisoners; but the strong guard, at the entrance, always baffled their attempts, and drove off the assailants with good-humored blows and laughter. As the arms of the drinkers had been taken from them, little danger was to be apprehended, unless they should succeed in obtaining them again. Night came on, and by the light of the fires the revellers carried on their orgies. The blaze falling on the front of the council-lodge, cast the rear and the

12 *

tents behind it into a dark shadow. Most of the inhabitants had gathered in the open space, and were occupied in observing the mad antics of the drunken Indians. At length, while the carousing was at its height, a figure slowly emerged from the edge of the forest, and keeping in the darkest shadows, outstretched upon the ground, coiled along slowly and cautiously towards the lodge. There it rolled up close beside the lower logs of the rude building, and even to a searching eye was almost indistinguishable from them. Thus it lay for some time motionless. Le Loup had just stretched himself upon the hard floor, when he heard a low sound like the ticking of an insect in the log near his head. It persevered in a singular manner, and he answered it with a like sound.

"Huron!" said a voice very low, but perfectly distinct—reaching no other ear but that of the prostrate warrior.

"Le Loup!" replied the other, giving his name.

"Good!" said the other voice, which the Huron recognized as that of Ahasistari.

"Council to-night?" asked the chief after a pause.

" No ; to-morrow ! " said Le Loup.

" Is the blackgown strong enough to travel to
the river ? "

" Yes ! but the Mohawk is quick and watchful."

" Can the Huron escape from the lodge with
the help of Ahasistari ? "

" There is an opening above, but all are bound
hand and foot."

" The knife of Ahasistari will sever the cord "
—a silence ensued, during which the chief was
busily occupied in removing a block, which filled
up the space between two of the logs — " let Le
Loup lay close, so that the knife may cut his
cord," said Ahasistari, as the block began to
yield to his efforts. At this moment two braves
of the guard, fearful that some of the carousers
might endeavor to do mischief through an opening in the rear, passed around the lodge to examine it. They conversed as they went along, and
the engrossing topic of the village expectation
filled their minds.

" The pale-face is a great medicine," said one ;
" the braves of the tribe will not spare him in
the council — for he will blight the coming har-
vest, and cast a spell on the hunting-grounds."

" The big Huron will be tortured," said the other.

" Yes! no one will adopt them, and they must ↓ be tortured, the dogs! "

"The council will decide to-morrow — Kiohba wishes all to be tortured. None know the wishes of Kiodego, and the war-chief is silent."

The two Mohawks now stood for a moment almost touching Ahasistari, who lay close to the side of the lodge, motionless as the wood itself. From their conversation the chief gathered that the council was looked to with great anxiety, as there was a diversity of opinion with regard to the fate of the Jesuit. At this moment a wild yell interrupted the two Mohawks, and drew them away. The carousers having exhausted the liquor set out for them, searched for the remainder, and having found it, overpowered the guard and bore it off. The Huron chief renewed his efforts with more hardihood, when he was again interrupted. The Indians in charge of the lodge had left it unprotected, and hastened to the assistance of their companions. Several of the half intoxicated Mohawks discovered this, and rushed towards the lodge in a body, determined to sacrifice the prisoners upon the instant. The old women had obtained some of the rum, and now, intoxicated, they joined furiously in the revels, till the open space around the fires presented a scene worthy of pandemonium. The light of the fires, as they stirred and tossed up the brands, flashed fitfully upon the crowds of reeling wretches, shrieking in the madness of inebriety. Here were groups contending with the guards for the last remnants of the fire-water. There parties of the revellers fought and struggled in harmless fury among themselves. The grave and solemn Indian warrior was transformed into a wallowing brute; some sat, like grinning idiots, gazing with meaningless faces into the fires, whose glare played wildly over their crouching figures — whilst, fiercest of all, came on towards the lodge, the few bent on murder. They had reached the opening, no guards were there; the fastenings were yielding to their hands. At that moment a powerful figure rose up, as it were in the midst of them, and mingled with them. Two heavy blows from his stalwart arm brought the foremost of the rioters to the ground; the rest fell over them shouting madly. The figure drew back behind the corner of the lodge, for the cries of the party had attracted the guard, who ran in strength to the spot, and having relieved the prisoners from danger, which was imminent, remained doubly watchful at their position. In a moment more Ahasistari gained the edge of the forest and stood awaiting the result. All hope of escape for that night was cut off. Some of the guards took their position within the lodge, while others destroyed the rum that still remained, as the only means of quieting the tumult; and one by one the revellers fell off into the deep sleep of intoxication.

Ahasistari returned to his hiding-place among the rocks, satisfied that no further harm would befall the prisoners until the council should decide upon their fate. Of the doom of Father Laval and Le Loup he felt little doubt, and he could delay no longer in the attempt at rescue, but must at length cast all his hope upon the hazard of the die. He must win all or lose all. As Quickfoot did not return, he concluded that he must have fallen in with Watook, and that they awaited his commands at the appointed spot. It was now necessary to dispatch the remaining Huron instantly to bring up these warriors, and, it would even then occupy them until the evening of the next day to reach the rocky hiding-place of their chief. The Huron set out, and Ahasistari was left alone. He knelt and prayed.

Father Laval remained some time absorbed in prayer after all the sounds without had died away. Of a strong and enduring frame, and used to hardships, he had already recovered from the effects of the long and painful march through the forest, while the novice, though much improvéd, still suffered severely from his labors. The Hurons, all along, aware that their chief was hovering about them, knew that any attempt at rescue was of too doubtful result for them to rest a hope upon, and prepared themselves still more, every hour, for that final and fatal trial which impended over them. At length they gave themselves up to slumber with cheerful hearts, trusting in the goodness and mercy of God.

With morning began the preparations for the council. The sullen countenances of those who had shared over night in the debauch, boded ill for the prisoners. Many a scowling and savage look was cast upon them. A little after noon came the deputation from the neighboring village: it was small, composed of but two or three braves, the greater portion of the successful warriors having gone out with their share of the plunder towards Fort Orange to exchange it for powder, lead, rum, and other articles of traffic. The deputies were received with much pomp and ceremony, and regaled with the best fare that the village contained. They were then conducted to the council-lodge, where the proceedings were opened with great state and solemnity. The elder and most distinguished braves formed themselves in a circle in the centre of the lodge; beyond them sat the less notable of the tribe. Each one, as he entered, took his seat in order; profound silence reigned throughout the assemblage. At length the old chief arrived — the calumet was passed around — and, at a sign from Kiodego, as a mark of honor, the brave who had commanded the successful war-posts arose to address them. His voice, at first low, swelled out as he proceeded, and his gesture became animated and picturesque. A robe of light skins was fastened around his waist and fell below his thigh; a collar, of the claws of the wild bear, hung around his neck; a snake-skin encircled his arm, and the feathers of the wild eagle adorned his head. His face was hideously painted. Streaks of black and red were drawn from his ears towards his mouth, while a broad band of vermilion extended across his forehead and over his eyes. As he spoke he pointed towards the prisoners, and at length singled out the Jesuit.

"Why has he come from his far land, from the bones of his fathers, across the great water, to the hunting-grounds of the red men? His people have settled down among our brothers in the north, and lo! they have made them women! They have turned the Hurons to dogs, made them forsake the Great Spirit, and join with the pale-face in battle against their own kind and color! The blackrobe is a medicine; he speaks, and warriors weep; the Hurons are his slaves;

13   K

he is a great medicine. What shall be the fate of the pale-face?"

The chief sat down, and a silence of a few minutes' duration ensued. It was broken at length by a warrior, who said:

"Let him die! Kiohba's voice is that the pale-face die at the stake. His enchantments have destroyed the Hurons, have driven away the buffalo and bounding deer. His people have swept down the beautiful forests on the great river. Kiohba has seen him make that sign upon his forehead, which our white brothers of Fort Orange tell us is a folly and a wickedness —a sorcery. If the chiefs spare the pale-face, he will soften the hearts of the Iroquois and weaken their arms in battle, and they will fall before his people, and become slaves, like the Hurons. The pale-face must die!"

Several of the warriors nodded their heads in silent approval of the speech of the brave.

"Let us keep the great medicine," said one who had not been of the war-party, but who had listened with wonder to the reported conversations of the priest. "Let us keep him in the tribe. Let us make him our brother, and give him the first ripe corn and the fattest of the deer! Let us build him a lodge, and his heart will love the Mohawk people, he will strengthen their arms and protect their villages!"

A smile of scorn played upon the lips of Kiohba, as he replied: "My brother is a cunning counsellor; he is wise and brave at the council-fire! Does he need a great medicine to strengthen his courage? Kiohba fears not the medicine. He has met the Huron and the French in battle. The pale-face must die!"

Other warriors now arose, some espousing one side and some the other. The dispute grew warm, when Kiodego interposed:

"My brothers!" he said, "it has been demanded, why the blackrobe came into our land, and why he goes far into the wilderness with the Hurons, scattering his spells upon his path. Let the pale-face answer! Unbind him, and lead him forward." A young warrior hastened to release the Jesuit, and assisted him into the circle.

"Speak, Tulhasaga!"* said the old chief

* "Morning-light inhabitants."

coldly, as if he had as yet heard nothing from the priest concerning the object of his mission. "Speak! Why comest thou to our land? What dost thou seek?"

Father Laval bowed his head for a moment in prayer, and then replied:

"Chief, I seek souls; I came to do the work of my Master; I came to preach another faith in this land, to teach and instruct the ignorant. My mission is one of peace; it is with the souls of men, and not their bodies. I would teach them to calm their passions, to cast out the spirit of evil from their hearts; to walk in the path of justice and of virtue. I came over the stormy waters to bear the tidings of the Gospel to the heathen, and to plant the holy cross in the wilderness. You ask, with what object I was going far into the west. I was about to seek new converts to the cross. But, chief," — and the voice of the missionary swelled out into its fullest and most musical tones, entrancing the ear of the savage. His form was lifted up, and his hands outstretched before him. "But, chief, the Great Spirit, in his wisdom, has willed it otherwise.

From my path to the Huron country he has turned my steps towards the Mohawk villages — and here, O chief, in captivity, submissive to the will of my divine Master, I preach Christ to the Iroquois; I preach Christ crucified; listen to me!" Deep exclamations broke from the astonished council, but they awaited in patience. "You are in darkness, I bring you light! receive it!" And he told them how God had created the world, and man the lord of all; of the fall; of the redemption; of the new Gospel; of the commission to his apostles and their successors, to go forth and "teach all nations, baptizing them in the name of the Father, and of the Son, and of the Holy Ghost;" how that commission had been sealed by miracles; how the blind saw, the lame walked, and the dead were raised to life again. And then he painted before their eyes, in glowing colors, the joys of heaven which were reserved for those who should believe in *Him*, and love and serve Him, and the fearful torments which the all-just God destined for those who should reject and disobey His commands. A gleam of wild joy broke from the

13*

eyes of the Hurons, as they looked upon the astonished Mohawks, while the Jesuit continued: "This is the religion which I preach; these are the glad tidings which I bring you; and it is to announce this Gospel to the children of the wilderness that I have come from the land of the east. The Great Spirit speaks it to you by my mouth; listen, and believe!"

Father Laval concluded, and silence reigned for a time throughout the lodge. At length Kiodego addressed him:

"My brother has spoken well, he is wise! But he tells a strange tale, how shall we believe him?"

"He speaks with a forked tongue," said Kiohba; "he is a liar!"

"We are satisfied with our own God," exclaimed another — "the war-god — Wacondah. The God of the great medicine has made cowards of the Hurons; the God of the Mohawks strengthens the arms of his children in battle. The Mohawks want not the God of the paleface." And then the clamor for his death became louder, while the advocates, not of mercy, but of delay for expediency, were silenced. The

fate of the good priest seemed already sealed.
Without further delay, a Mohawk approached
him, and, at a signal from the chief, compelled
him to kneel, and began to paint his head and
face. Then a shout of joy broke from the crowd
without; for it was the mark of death upon the
victim, and they revelled already in anticipation
of the torture. At that moment a slight movement was made in the crowd around the door; it
swayed forward and backward, and then gave
way, leaving an opening into the centre of the
circle. Leaning upon a warrior, Kiskepila,
weak and tottering, with his bandages still upon
his wounds, pressed forward through the passage.
The eye of the young chief fell upon the group
in the centre. An exclamation burst from his
lips. With the mighty energy of a strong spirit
he rose from the arm that supported his weak
form and strode alone into the circle. With one
hand he cast aside the Mohawk; the other he
rested upon the brow of the priest. A death-like
stillness reigned upon the scene; not a hand was
raised to arrest his course; not a voice was uplifted against him. Surprise held all men silent,

while the flashing eye of the young warrior
turned from face to face. "Kiskepila is a chief,"
said the young eagle of his tribe, "who will
oppose him? The Hurons have fled before the
arm of Kiskepila! Shall he have no voice in
the councils of the tribe?" And he placed the
other hand above the head of the kneeling priest.
"Shall he be silent when the boaster is heard?"
and he pointed to Kiohba. "Kiskepila asks
the chiefs and braves to spare the pale-face." He
looked around for a reply — there was none. At
length Kiohba said coldly :

"The chiefs and braves have spoken ; the pale-
face must die. See! the death-paint is upon his
brow."

With a look of scorn the young man turned
away from the speaker and glanced once more
around the circle. The features of the stern
Mohawks were unmoved; they were silent.
Kiohba was triumphing.

"My brothers!" said Kiskepila, his eye lighting up again with indignation, "my brothers,
Kiskepila was wounded and fainting, and dying
upon the field of battle; and the pale-face bathed

his lips and bound his wounds. Kiskepila owes a life to the pale-face, and he will repay it. Let Kiohba show the mark of a Huron on his breast, or the scalp of a foe at his girdle."

The Indian replied not. The eyes of the old men turned upon the Jesuit, and, with an exclamation of wonder, they looked to the chief of the war-party, for confirmation of a story to them so strange.

"The words of the young eagle are true," he said; "the pale-face bound up the wounds of Kiskepila; he saved his life. The blackrobe was a dove upon the field of battle—a dove among the eagles."

Silence again ensued. The Jesuit, wrapped in prayer, scarce heeded the scene around him; but ever and anon the bright eye of Le Loup would gleam upon him, as, with head bent forward, the Huron listened, with interest, to the words of the young Mohawk chief.

"The council have spoken!" said Kiohba again, fearful that a change might take place in the opinions of the warriors, some of whom seemed to lean towards the young chief; "the council have spoken; the pale-face must die. It is right; for the spells of the blackrobe are upon the heart of Kiskepila; he has made a Huron of the Mohawk."

"You lie, dog!" exclaimed the young chief, fiercely.

"The tongue of Kiohba is not forked," said the other, coldly, feeling the advantage which he was gaining, through the generous impetuosity of his opponent. "Let the chiefs look: Kiskepila could not walk alone to the council-lodge; and see! he stands, as if he had no wounds upon him; it is the spell of the pale-face medicine. The blackrobe must die, or the warriors will become women!"

The old men shook their heads, as they looked upon the upright and noble figure of the young brave, while the bandages were still fresh, as it were, upon deep and dangerous wounds. It was the energy of the spirit, not of the flesh, that sustained the chief. The eyes of Kiohba gleamed with joy, as he saw the impression he had made. The young man again spoke, but in a lower and sterner tone:

"Kiskepila owes the pale-face a life; he shall not die! Kiskepila will adopt him as his brother, in place of him who is dead. He demands the pale-face for his brother!"

Kiohba smiled grimly, as he replied, pointing to the old chief: "The father may demand the prisoner, to adopt him as his son. Let the chief speak; will he take to his lodge the sorcerer, who has changed the heart of the young eagle who was *once* the truest of the Mohawks?"

Absorbed in anxious expectation, the young brave heeded not the taunt. The old man was silent for a moment, then raising his head, replied firmly:

"Kiskepila *was* a warrior, a Mohawk. He has taken a Huron heart. The pale-face has told him strange tales, and he has heard. The blackgown is a sorcerer. The father of Kiskepila will not claim him; let him die!" The head of the young chief sunk upon his breast, and he was silent.

"He must die!" re-echoed Kiohba, and, tauntingly, continued: "He tells you that his God raised the dead to life; why does he not call up the great Champlain from the tomb to protect his people? Let us see whether his God will save the pale-face, when the flames shall glow and curl around his white limbs!'"

"You demand of me a miracle!" Father Laval replied gently; "you call on my God to raise the dead. He has done so; he can do it again. He has opened the silent tomb, and bid the dead arise and come forth, glowing with life, and health, and energy; and he has done this at the prayer of his holy servants. I am but his humble follower. What right have you to demand from the God who made you, a sign and a miracle in testimony? Yours is not the prayer of the willing; it is the scoff of the hater."

The indignant voice of the Jesuit ceased. After a pause of some moments an Indian approached, and finished painting his head and face. It was the sign of final condemnation, and was received with exultation by many; yet there were not a few who began to entertain an increased dread of what they imagined to be his power. But the feeling of the council was

excited, although that assemblage still retained·
its calm and grave aspect; and, with but little
delay, the novice and the Hurons were also con-
demned to the torture.   Father Laval, Le Loup
and two other Hurons were to suffer on the morrow, in front of the council-lodge, while Rene
Bourdoise and the three remaining Hurons were
to be tortured at the other village.   The prisoners received their doom calmly, the Hurons
looking coldly on the preparations, which were
begun at once, to carry out the sentence of the
council, which then broke up.

When Kiskepila found all his efforts fruitless,
he took the arm of the warrior, who had assisted
him to the spot, for his strength began to fail
very rapidly, and, in silence, returned to his
tent, determined not to look upon sufferings
which he could not prevent or alleviate.   Morning Flower awaited sadly the termination of the
council, and wept over the fate of the blackgown; but she recalled to memory the beautiful
lessons of patience which he had taught her, and
suppressed the manifestation of her grief.

The Huron messenger of Ahasistari struck
14

directly through the forest in the direction of the place where the braves were supposed to lie concealed. The stars were shining in the clear heavens, and an occasional glance at their sparkling orbs served to guide his path. Up over hill and steep ascent, over swamp and morass went the swift Indian, at his leaping trot, tireless, never pausing. Midnight came, and the runner still pressed on; his moccasined feet springing yet lightly from the soft turf, as he bounded on. Darkness melted slowly into the gray of morn, and morning brightened into day, and yet the Huron speeded on. At length he paused upon the summit of a little hill. At its foot, clear and pellucid, flowed a gentle stream. But no trace could he discover of any living thing upon its banks, or in its surrounding forest. A moment more his eye scanned the wood, and then descended to the water's edge. As he leaned upon his rifle, he carefully observed the current flowing by him, till his gaze seemed riveted by a floating twig, with green leaves upon it. An eddy whirled it in towards the shore, and he drew it towards him with the butt of his rifle.

The fracture of the branch was fresh, and it was evidently torn, not bitten off. Swinging his rifle into the hollow of his arm, the runner turned directly up the stream, taking care to leave no tracks behind him. For some time he proceeded on his course, still casting an occasional glance at the forest around him, and on the ground before him, watching for the marks of a trail. Suddenly he paused, and looked intently upon the ground, and then stooped down to examine the surface more closely.

" Hugh ! pale-face ! " he exclaimed.

The step was turned from the stream ; treading cautiously, so as not to obliterate the trail. He followed it back to the water's edge, and examined the bushes which grew there ; they were of the same kind as the branch which he held in his hand. Falling into the trail, he traced it up the hill, along the summit of which it ran. At length a low whistling struck upon his ear, and he paused to listen ; and then crept on more cautiously. At the foot of a large tree, on an elevated spot, from which an extensive sweep of the forest, facing towards the Mohawk village, was visible, sat the figure of a white man, holding in his hand a large rough ox-horn, which he was busily engaged in shaping into a powder-horn. Every now and then he compared it with the one which was slung at his side, and then renewed his labors. Suddenly a new idea seemed to strike him; and, putting it to his mouth, he gave a blast, which made the Huron start with surprise. Then he began at once to shape the small opening into something like a mouth-piece. At last he seemed satisfied, and putting it to his lips, sounded it again.

"Ha! that will do!" he said at length; "good idea; Indian hates the sound of a horn, and I like it. Well, I may want it soon;" and he stuck it in his belt. As he did so, the Huron runner stepped before him.

"L'Espion Hardi!" The scout sprang to his feet, grasping his rifle.

"Ah! Huron!" he said, as his eye fell upon the dress and paint of the Indian; and he resumed his seat again.

"Huron? Yes! No Mohawk! or"—and the Indian pointed significantly to his scalp.

"Right, Huron! I was making a powder-horn, when I thought of the trumpets of Champlain, as he marched to battle: Ah! did you ever fight under Champlain, Huron?"

"No! the chief and many of the braves were out!"

"Yes, I know it, Huron! Well, it came into my head to try how a good blast would sound in this old forest. It was rash, I won't deny it," he continued, as the Huron shook his head; "but a Frenchman loves the sound of the trumpet. Listen now," he said, applying the trumpet to his lips once more; but the Indian placed his hand upon it and said:

"Daring scout! Mohawk hunter may hear!"

"Yes, yes! but when we were out against the Mohawks with Champlain, he let them hear more of it than they liked."

"Great brave!" said the runner.

"Yes, *he* was a warrior! It does me good to hear his name shouted in a brisk charge; it helps wonderfully, although he is dead and gone now. Yes, he was a man," continued Pierre, sorrowfully; "no such man in all the province

now, or these rascally Mohawks would be taught
a lesson worth remembering."

"The daring scout is with the Huron braves?"
asked the runner.

"Yes! and I suppose you are the messenger
that I am to look for?"   The runner nodded his
head, and the other continued:

"They are across the stream; let us go;" and,
swinging his rifle over his shoulder, the scout
descended the hill with rapid strides.   When
they approached the stream, the runner glided to
the side of the hunter, and holding up the broken
twig before him, said:

"Daring scout casts a trail upon the water.
Huron found this far down the stream."

The scout looked at it for a moment, while the
runner explained himself; and then, half angry
at the implied reproach, answered:

"Well, and but for that twig you would not
have found us; you missed the trail!"

"I crossed it in the night," said the Huron,
"but not far off.   Up or down the stream, the
Huron would soon have found it."

"Far enough, at any rate," said the scout,

"or you would have been here at once, without striking on the stream below. See, here is one of Quickfoot's marks upon this oak; *he* followed directly upon the trail, and even made it plainer, for you, by these gashes!"

"Bad!" replied the runner quickly; "Mohawk keen eye!"

"Night and day," continued the scout, "we kept watch, by turns, upon that hill which overlooked the path, waiting for the messenger, whom Quickfoot told us Ahasistari would send."

"Huron!" said Pierre, after walking some time in silence, "have you seen the prisoners?"

"Yes, from the woods; saw blackgown walking about."

"Well, perhaps then they won't attempt to kill them yet, and we can get there in time."

The Indian shook his head, and said:

"To-day council; to-morrow torture; daring scout knows how it is."

"Then," said the scout sternly, as he strode along with swifter step, "then, Huron, there will be at the dance some guests not invited."

They hastened on in silence, until they reached

the place of concealment. It was well chosen.
In an extensive thicket, a space had been cut
away, and here the warriors were lying about in
groups upon their blankets. Exclamations of
delight welcomed the scout and the runner, and
the whole body assembled in council. The runner explained the condition of things, and delivered the order of the chief; and in a few moments
more the party, nineteen in number, took up their
line of march, throwing out active scouts in advance, to guard against any accidental meeting
with the Mohawks.

CHAPTER X.

THE TORTURE.

IMMEDIATELY after the breaking up of the council, the Mohawks began their preparations for the coming festival. Four stakes were planted in front of the lodge, and piles of fagots were gathered in the forest. At a little distance beyond the first, four other stakes were placed, to which the prisoners, whose fate was postponed, were to be bound, that they might witness the agony of their brethren, and suffer, themselves, in anticipation. The youths of the village now commenced to gather about the lodge, in order to enjoy the preliminary torture, which was permitted them for their own especial amusement, and to practise them in the ways of cruelty. This sometimes endured until taken

part in by the braves, when it did not cease until
death brought relief to the victim. Le Loup
and Father Laval were brought forth and tied to
two of the stakes, and the clamorous mob hovered around them, pelting and annoying them in
a thousand ingenious modes of petty torture.
They soon, however, became more systematic,
and, drawing off to a little distance, practised
upon their living targets, with the bow and
arrow, and the tomahawk. Le Loup stood up
with the proud and fearless bearing of the warrior, his steady eye gleaming unmoved upon the
flashing weapon, as, hurled from the skilful
hand, it grazed his temple, and sank quivering
into the post behind him. Another and another
threw; it was a desperate game, in which the
winner was he who came nearest to death without touching life. Father Laval endured with
the meekness and patience of the martyr; his
eyes were upturned to heaven, for he dared not
look upon the hand that threw the coming
weapon. Kiohba, the Mohawk, stretched out
upon the soft turf, watched the youthful tormentors with quiet enjoyment, occasionally sug-

gesting to them some new mode of increasing the
sufferings of the victims. At length, as his appetite for cruelty became excited, he arose, and,
seizing one of the tomahawks, drew back and
hurled it at the Jesuit. The weapon whistled
through the air, and struck the post by his temple, driving a lock of his hair into the wood. A
shout of delight arose from the crowd at this
evidence of skill, and Kiohba, raising another
weapon, aimed a second time at the priest. It
struck upon the other side as truly as the first,
and the victim stood drawn back to the post by
his own hair. Renewed applause broke from
the youths, and each one endeavored to emulate
the skill of the warrior. After some time they
grew tired of their sport, and the prisoners were
permitted for a while to remain unmolested.

As the crowd drew away from the spot, the
figure of a maiden glided silently to the side of
the Jesuit, and, offering a cooling draught to his
parched lips, bathed his brow, which the intense
excitement had caused to throb with feverish
pain.

"Stranger from over the far waters, Morning

Flower thought once to avenge upon thee the wounds of the Young Eagle. But blackgown has pardoned the wrongs of the Mohawk girl. Thou hast told us of the glory of forgiving and loving our enemies — Tulhasaga, thou art the enemy of the Mohawks, but Morning Flower doth not hate thee."

"Heaven bless thee, my child, and lead thee, through the merits of Him who died upon the cross, to the way of salvation, preserving thee from trials and sufferings," said the Jesuit, sadly but fervently.

The Indian girl placed herself upon the grass and looked up into his face affectionately, as if to a father, and said, as she caught the mournful expression upon the countenance of the priest:

"Blackgown, thou hast told me that each one shall bear his cross, as the Saviour, of whom thou speakest, bore his. Blackgown, thou art bound unto thy cross!"

In a moment, the sad expression passed from the features of the Jesuit, and, with a holy enthusiasm, he exclaimed:

"Oh God! in the midst of sorrow and tribu-

lation, thou dost send down consolations un-
speakable to thy servant; by the mouth of this
wild maiden, thou hast uttered to me words of
sweet and saving import; thou hast strengthened
me; thou hast consoled. Oh! how happy to
bear my cross, to suffer—to suffer for thy sake!
Gentle maiden—woman still! woman who did
not shrink from the cross and its ignominy, from
the shouts and curses of the crucifiers! woman,
still the faithful and the pure, and the unswerv-
ing! woman, the holy, holy from the holiness of
the stainless mother, pure from the purity of the
immaculate, gentlest of God's creatures—it was
given to thee to be the angel of mercy and the
comforter of the afflicted. Kind maiden, thou
hast soothed the sad spirit; may the mother most
pure, the ennobler of thy sex, the ever virgin,
intercede for thee."

And then the spirit of the captive seemed
wrapt in meditation, and he stood, with eyes cast
upwards, and lips moving silently. A holy and
tranquil glow crept softly over the face of him
who awaited a death of horrible torture. Sweetly
it grew upon that countenance, the beam of

15

prayer, and hope, and joy, spreading from feature to feature, till nothing of earth was left. Upwards, upwards soared the soul upon the wings of love; upwards until it seemed already to be mingling its whispered orisons with the seraphic choir. Hast thou looked upon the sunlight stealing gently o'er a shadowed spot? Hast thou marked the sombre cloud disperse, until nothing but the glad skies looked down upon thee? Hast thou watched the shrouding mist evanish, or the pale hue of sickness brighten into the red glow of health? Thus fled sorrow and sadness from the captive's face.

The untutored maiden looked in wonder on the change wrought, as it were, by one unconscious word. Here she sat, looking fondly up to that glorious, heavenly face, catching from its pure mirror a reflection of holy thought. Unconscious the Jesuit stood, visions of bliss hovered around him; the gentle zephyr that fanned his cheek seemed beaten on it by the wings of seraphs; joyous songs broke upon his ear, and clouds of incense floated sweetly over his wrapt senses. Death and torture were before him, but

heaven was above him: could he look down-
wards to the earth and its fleeting torments? O
wonderful mission of Christianity! which came
upon earth to raise man far above the very sub-
limest idea of the heathen God, to inspire him
with thought above the power of mortality, to
give him a life which death could not extinguish
—a life beyond and above this earth—a ray of
the Spirit of God. Still unmoved the Jesuit
stood, his head thrown back and resting upon
the stake, his body supported by the cords which
bound him, every function slumbering, every
energy absorbed. He was in truth only an im-
prisoned soul. Welcome the knife, welcome the ·
torture, welcome death by fire, by steel, by slow
delay, for the spirit is away upon its wings, already soaring in pre-enjoyment with the blessed.
What are a few short hours of suffering to the
eternity of such bliss? Oh yes! *now* welcome,
Death! for thou canst only be the usher of
eternal life!

Like the shadow, when the sunbeam has passed,
came back the thought of earth to the soul of the
priest. A deep sigh broke from his half closed
lips:

"How long! O Lord! how long!"

Awe-stricken sat the simple Indian maiden, as she gazed upon that countenance effulgent with ineffable happiness, glowing with unearthly beauty. With parted lips and fixed eye, she gazed reverently—for woman, blessed as the instrument of the great blessing to man, catches intuitively the beam of heaven's light, and reflects it in her soul.

"Mary—!" exclaimed the Jesuit, and the broken aspiration was finished unheard.

"Mary!" repeated the Indian maiden, in her soft and musical accents. "Mary!" There was prayer in that whispered word—prayer of the soul—and it arose from the wild heart of the untutored Indian—from the soul of the ecstatic priest—"Mary!"

At that moment came, swelling from the prison-house of the captive Hurons, the sound of a Christian hymn. From deep stern voices came it, but the melody was sad and plaintive, and varied with the varying measure of the rude, unpolished verse.

Hear mother, hear!
Hear, Queen of the bright and blessed!
  Now that death is near,
The prayer to thee addressed!
    Hear, for the day is flying,
    And thy poor children, sighing,
    Beseech thy aid in dying.
             Hear mother, hear!

    Mother of mercy, hear!
The sun on earth is sinking;
  With mingled hope and fear,
Thy children's hearts are shrinking;
    Mother, heed the suffering child,
    Beaten, wounded, bruised, reviled,
    Tortured in the forest wild.
             Mother, mother hear!

    Mother, by His blood!
Mother, by thy tears and sorrow,
  By the earth's redeeming wood,
Aid us in our strife to-morrow!
    Win from thy all-conquering Son,
    By the triumph he has won,
    Grace and strength to gain our own.
            Mother, mother hear!

Softly hushed the sound of prayer, and the
notes died away, but the still form of the Indian
15 *

girl scarce moved — waiting for the deep-toned music to awake again. It came not, and she murmured in the air, "Mother, mother hear!"

The haughty bearing of Le Loup had passed away; the keen eye, that had gazed unmoved upon the flashing tomahawk, was dimmed and softened; his head rested upon his breast. He was wrapt in prayer. He was the savage warrior no longer, but the Christian.

At length, from the council-lodge came faintly swelling the voice of the young novice, and alternately responding the full chorus of the Hurons. They were reciting the litany. Sadly struck the tones of his young companion's voice upon the ear of the Jesuit. They were weak and tremulous. Morning Flower listened — was it the warrior's death-song? Never before, in the villages of her tribe, had such chant been raised by those who were about to die. The Jesuit and Le Loup joined in the responses, and the solemn "*Miserere nobis*" rose distinct and clear. The maiden hung in wrapt attention on the alternate sounds of many voices mingling in heartfelt prayer. Thus passed the autumn sunset.

Ahasistari sat alone in his rocky hiding-place.
Ever and anon he cast a meaning glance towards
the west, where the sky was yet tinged with gold,
although the orb of day had disappeared. Then
he rested his head upon his knees and remained
immovable. His rifle lay at his feet, and his
remaining arms upon it, as if he had just been
preparing them carefully for immediate use.
Twilight came, still the chief moved not. At
length he arose, and approaching the entrance of
the cavern, looked out upon the forest, listening
intently for some welcome sound — nothing struck
upon his ear save the rustling of the leaves and
the low swinging of the overhanging branches.
There was silence in the vast forest; the hum of
the little insect, as it uttered its evening prayer,
was the only sound of living thing that broke
upon the solitude. For a moment it seemed that
a shadow of doubt passed across the brow of the
warrior. It occurred to him that his party might
have been cut off. He could not doubt but that
Watook had collected a force and followed in
pursuit; and that Quickfoot, his first messenger,
had fallen in with them, as otherwise the saga-

cious Huron would have returned days ago, to
share the fortunes of his chief. Perhaps his last
messenger had missed the trail in the forest, and
for a time the chief almost regretted that he had
not dared the risk consequent upon the concealment of so many men near the village, accompanied, as it was, with the advantage of their
proximity in case a sudden opportunity of rescue
presented itself. It was already time that the
party should have reached the place of his concealment which he had designated as the point
of rendezvous. But hours might yet elapse
before the torture would begin, for although he
did not know the exact result of the council's
deliberations, he felt that there was little doubt
of the condemnation of Father Laval and the
other prisoners; and that their lives hung upon
a thread liable to be broken at any moment by
the whim or caprice of the savages. As he cast
his eye around, indistinctly it caught the radiance
of a stream of light illuminating the mist that
hung above the village. Taking up his arms he
descended to the forest below, and a few moments'
walk brought him to a place whence he could

catch a glimpse of the lodges, and at the same time be near the path to the rendezvous. The glare of a large fire flashed up towards the darkening sky, and tinged with red the waving branches of the forest. Two figures were still bound to the stakes, and groups of boys and men were loitering about, seemingly awaiting some approaching event.

"The Hurons must speed on, or they will come too late," exclaimed Ahasistari bitterly, as he stretched himself upon the ground.

The fire flashed out more brightly now, for some hand had cast more fuel on it; and the light of the flame played around the mild face of the Jesuit as he stood bound to the stake. His high, bold forehead seemed to catch the floating beams, which lingered round it, like a saintly halo of coming glory. Ahasistari recognized the form of Father Laval, even at that distance, and, looking for a moment in silence, exclaimed:

"They will come too late! there will be one more stake and one more torture! My father, I swear to thee that Ahasistari will share thy fortunes, whether of death or life!" and he arose

M

and turned towards the village. Suddenly he
paused, and cast his eyes to the northeast as if he
would penetrate the dark veil that stretched before
him; then he laid his ear to the very ground and
listened. At length casting his rifle upon the sod,
he sat down, and shrouding his face in his hands,
remained still and motionless as a statue.

It seemed as if the Mohawks were about to
anticipate the hour of final torture. The prisoners were brought out, one by one, and bound
to the stakes until the eight were occupied. The
crowd began to increase, and new fires were
raised. The women gathered the fagots nearer.
Father Laval looked sadly upon these preparations; but the Huron, Le Loup, perceiving what
was passing in his mind, said in broken French:

"Not yet, my father, not yet. The Mohawk
is not so merciful! he loves hours of torture!"

"Oh God! give us grace to die worthily!"
exclaimed the Jesuit, and then resumed his silent
prayer.

Darkness was deepening, but the lights of the
blazing fires rushed up fitfully to heaven, casting
a red gleam upon the scene around, and making

the ferocious Mohawks, as they flitted about in
their fell work, resemble so many fiends at their
infernal orgies. The prisoners were stripped of
their clothing, and the work of torture began.
Snatching up burning pieces of wood, the
savages held them close to the naked skin until
its surface blistered with the slow heat; then, as
the swollen part became dead and senseless to the
lesser torture, they pressed the live coal into the
raw flesh until it hissed, and fumed, and cracked,
while the groan of intense agony arose from the
lips of the white sufferers. The stern Indian
endured in silence. Father Laval, as the red
cinders pierced his flesh, elevated his soul to
God, and dwelt upon the sufferings of him whose
brow had borne a crown of thorns, whose hands
and feet had been torn with nails, whose precious
side had been opened with a spear. "Jesus,
Mary, and Joseph," were ever on his lips, and
his upraised spirit seemed at last to forsake and
leave behind it the sorrow and sufferings of earth;
and to float already upwards through a sea of
ineffable delights.

Rene Bourdoise, reserved for future death, did

not escape from present torture. His tormentors surrounded him, and forced into his tender skin small splinters of pitch-pine, and, when a number had been pressed in thus, they applied blazing torches to the parts which obtruded, and the dark flame ran swiftly, from one to another, along the bristling surface, until it became a mass of fire. In vain the suffering youth struggled to escape; his bands only permitted him to wind round and round the stake; but, whichever way he turned, blows met him or blazing knots of pine. Thus eight victims suffered—ten thousand deaths were they enduring, and yet so skilful was the Indian in his torture that death itself could not relieve them. The novice, weak from his long fatigues, yet sore from former wounds and sufferings, at length became exhausted, and hung supported by his bands alone. Father Laval, moving in the midst of his tortures around the stake, began to pray aloud:

"The pale-face warrior sings his death-song," said Kiobba, "how many warriors hath he slain? How many scalps has he taken? He is a woman! a slave! a dog!" and the shouts

of the infuriated mob drowned the voice of
the priest.

In the tent of Kiodego, the chief, sat a
wounded man, faint and weak; his form reclined
against a pile of furs, his hands covered his face,
his breathing was deep and stern, but there was
no other mark of life about him. At his feet
sat an Indian maiden — Morning Flower was
weeping!

Still on rang the furious shout of the wild
savage — on went the fearful torture — the fiendish dance went on. But loudest of all arose
above the tumult the shrill voices of the beldames
as they gathered around Le Loup. The Indian
heeded them not; he was preparing himself to
die. Then for a time it seemed as if the frenzy
of the Mohawks was dying away, but it soon
broke out in renewed fury, and the various
crowds drew off to hurl the tomahawk.

"See," said Kiohba, "how a brave can
strike!" and he repeated the feat of skill he had
before performed. With a laugh of scorn, another Mohawk stepped forth, and brandishing
his weapon, exclaimed:

16

"You have grazed his head, I will drive the ears of the blackgown into the stake."

The Mohawk aimed at Father Laval, who gazed upon him almost unconsciously. The moment was one of deep peril; no matter how skilful the aim, a sudden motion of the victim, an involuntary start would, instead of mutilation, bring death. It was a feat of nice and precise skill, and the Mohawk measured his distance carefully, and drew back his arm.

Suddenly the peal of a rifle broke upon the air, and then another and another, in quick succession, flashed from the forest, and a wild and exulting shout broke out. Down came the fierce Mohawk — another and another fell — whilst the whole northern circle of the forest seemed blazing with continuous flashes. Hushed was the voice of the warrior — mute the shrill tongue of woman — terror-stricken, they clustered together. Their rifles, and bows and arrows were in their cabins; there was a scattering in wild affright to obtain their arms; one figure alone sprung towards the bound prisoners, tomahawk in hand.

Over the wild peal of battle rose the firm voice
of Ahasistari, and the Hurons sprung out from
their covers to the charge, to strike the effective
blow before the Mohawks could rally. Out from
the impenetrable darkness bounded these dusky
figures, rushing on, with wild and exulting
shouts, to cut off the entrance to the cabins;
one, a lithe and youthful form, shaking fiercely
over his head his small steel axe, leaped forward
to the prisoners. Watook was rushing to the
rescue.

Kiohba pressed on in his fell purpose. He
reached the side of the novice, he wound his
hand in his long hair, he bent back his head,
and, glaring fiendishly into his face, he seemed
to make him die by slow and fearful agony;
then his weapon flashed above him, and came
down with a sullen crash, and the form of the
poor novice sunk lifeless, supported by the withes
that bound him to the stake. Kiohba unwound
his hand from his locks, and tore the scalp from
his mangled brow; then he turned towards the
Jesuit. Le Loup struggled to burst his bands,
but his iron strength would not avail him; in

helpless agony he had looked on. At that moment a well-known voice was in his ear; a single heavy stroke severed the cord that bound him, and the tall Huron, tossing up his arms to heaven, as if glorying in the thought of freedom once again, sprung on to the rescue. The fierce Mohawk was already by the side of the priest; his arm was outstretched to aim the fatal blow, when Le Loup, like a wolf upon his prey, bounded on him. Down came the two powerful savages — the armed and the unarmed — but life and retribution nerved the heart of the Huron, and strung his sinews. The weapon of Kiohba was dashed from his grasp as he fell to the earth, and he sought for the knife in his girdle. For a moment it seemed doubtful which would conquer. Over and over, the two rolled swiftly upon the ground. At length the hand of Le Loup rested upon the knife of his foe; in a moment more it gleamed in the light, and was buried in the heart of the Mohawk. The strong grasp of Kiohba relaxed, and, casting off his nerveless hand, the Huron arose from the fearful struggle. So rapid had it been that the last prisoner was just released.

Father Laval cast himself upon his knees in prayer, while the Hurons caught up what arms they could find, and, headed by Le Loup, dashed on towards the spot where Ahasistari and his followers were contending with superior numbers. The blaze of the fires cast a fearful light upon the battle-scene, seeming to double the numbers of the combatants, and to swell their forms into gigantic size. Two powerful Mohawks were rushing towards their cabins for their arms; the chief of the Hurons intercepted them. The first attempted to close with him, but a single blow of the tomahawk stretched him lifeless at his feet: the second was upon him before he could recover from his effort, and aimed a stroke at his head. The Huron warded it skilfully, and they closed. The struggle was terrific, but was short, and Ahasistari, as he quitted the dead body of the Mohawk, cast a glance upon the scene of battle.

Fearful had been the first onslaught of the Hurons. They had met their foes; as in panic, they broke away towards their wigwams, and by the fury of their assault, had driven them back to the open space. Here they began to rally and

10 *

to fight with something of their accustomed
bravery. An Indian, taken by surprise, can sel-
dom recover, and the Mohawks waged an un-
equal battle with their fierce and determined
assailants; but for their superior numbers, the
rout would have been instantaneous and terrific.
They began to rally; the women, and children,
and old men appeared upon the scene, the women
bearing the rifles, and the bows and arrows of the
warriors. With renewed energy the Mohawks
fought, armed as they were with tomahawks and
clubs; scarcely a shot pealed upon the air, and,
in the stern battle of man to man, no cry broke
forth. Suddenly upon the stillness came the
loud blast of a horn from the southern portion of
the forest, echoing and re-echoing in the hills to
the north; then a terrific shout, and, high above
the rest, the battle-cry —"Champlain a nous!
Champlain!"

Sweeping down the sward rushed a band of
dark figures that seemed, in the flickering light,
of countless numbers, while the loud and deafen-
ing blast of the horn still rang on, and ever, as it
paused, the battle-cry, "Champlain! Champlain!" broke out.

The Mohawk warriors stood aghast. Had the dead really arisen? Had the great medicine accepted their challenge, and called the mighty warrior from his tomb to the rescue? Was it a ghastly troop, with horrible sounds of unearthly import, that came upon them? Their arms dropped nerveless, and they paused in their onslaught—whilst the Hurons renewed their exulting cries, and charged once more upon them. The fire now gleamed out fiercely, stirred by a passing breath of wind, and the fitful light discovered to the frightened Mohawks the face and form of a white man bounding forward, and waving his glistening blade above his head.

"Champlain! Champlain! Mohawk dogs!" shouted the figure in the Iroquois tongue, as he dashed into their midst, striking down the first he met, with his long and curved knife.

"The dead! the dead! Champlain!" exclaimed the paralyzed Mohawks, and broke away from the field of battle. Women and children, old men and warriors, mindful of the scenes of the council, fled wildly off, veiling

their eyes from him whom they believed to
have arisen from the tomb: still in their ears
rung the cry of "Champlain! Champlain!" and
the relentless Frenchman, with his band, smiting
right and left, pursued them. Terror lent wings
to their speed, and they scattered deep in the
forest.

By the homes of their early years—by the
council-fire, where their fathers had sat—upon
the turf where, in childhood's hours, they had
sported—still gathered a stern band of veteran
Mohawks. They were few in number—fewer
than their foes—but they were true and unyielding braves. For a moment, when the rout
began, the battle had ceased; and the two parties
now stood gazing at one another in fierce defiance. The Mohawks were armed with no
weapons but those of a hand-to-hand fight—
and Ahasistari, casting aside his rifle with a
noble generosity, sprung forward to meet his foe
upon an equality of arms. Knife in hand he
grappled with a warrior; the Hurons followed
his example, and for a moment there was seen a
struggling crowd of indistinguishable figures;

here and there, with a convulsive spring, some
form would cease its motion, and lie still and
silent as the sod it pressed. The rest still struggled on. At length, from out the melee crept an
unarmed savage, wounded, coiling himself slowly
along the ground as if in dying agony. He
reached the corner of the lodge, and passing behind its shadow, sprung quickly to his feet. His
eye fell upon the kneeling figure of Father Laval as he bent him over a dying Huron, and
tearing off a portion of his belt, he stole quietly
behind him. In a moment he had gagged him
— in another he was hurrying him rapidly, in
spite of his resistance, from the spot. The priest
attempted to cry out, but it was in vain; and
casting a lingering look towards the group where
his friends were fighting within reach of him —
yet ignorant of his danger — resigned himself to
his fate.

CHAPTER XI.

THE WREATH OF WILD FLOWERS.

AHASISTARI and his foes were struggling; the combat was fierce; but, one by
one, the Mohawks were overpowered or
slain, and the Hurons were left undisputed mas-
ters of the village. The noise of battle had
ceased; only the moan of pain broke the stillness
of the scene. Few, but the wounded and the
dead, were there besides themselves. Their chief
looked around in vain for the Jesuit and the
novice. He called out their names; they did not
answer. They searched the village; none were
there but the feeble, and those who were. unable
to flee. They turned in sorrow to the fires of
torture. Bound to his stake, supported almost
upright by his bands, like life but for the crushed
and bleeding brow, was the dead body of the

gentle novice. Softly they loosened the cords,
softly as if, even in death, they would not ruffle
the placid slumber of those pale and delicate
features. They laid him down upon the turf,
and sought again for the Jesuit. He was not
there. Catching up a burning brand, Ahasistari
examined the edge of the forest; suddenly he
uttered a low exclamation, and darted into its
depths. The glare of the torch, as its flame
tossed wildly in his swift course flitting past the
dark trunks of trees, looked like a red meteor in
its course.

. The Hurons silently gathered their dead from
the field, and laid them down by the body of the
young novice. Then they stood around them
solemnly. A few moments passed thus in stern
meditation; when, gliding noiselessly into the
group, and pressing aside the rest, two figures
approached close beside the body of the novice.
A low but joyful exclamation welcomed them.
Father Laval heeded it not. The steel axe,
which Ahasistari bore, was yet dripping with
warm blood; it told the Hurons the story of
the rescue. One by one came back the scattered
warriors from the pursuit, and, last of all, Le

Loup and Daring Scout. Father Laval knelt beside the body of his young companion; tears dimmed his eyes, and the voice of prayer, which arose from his lips for the departed spirit, came broken with sighs and indistinct with grief. Torches of blazing pine, placed by the silent Hurons at the head and feet of the dead, were sending up their bright flame, capped with dark clouds of smoke — fit emblem of the life of man. Around knelt the Christian warriors, mingling their prayers with those of the priest of God. The countenances of the Huron braves were stern and solemn; no other mark of grief appeared upon them. Kneeling at the feet of the departed were Le Loup and Watook, and behind them the stern scout. As he looked upon the pale features of the novice, a tear stole silently down his hard and weather-beaten face, and clung amid the scarred wrinkles until it mingled with the air, and arose to heaven, carrying with it, like perfume, to the skies the unspoken prayer of the melting heart. L'Espion Hardi was thinking of the gallant son whom he had thus buried in the forest. A hand touched him lightly upon the shoulder; when he looked up, Ahasistari stood beside him, and beckoned him to follow him. After they had gone some distance from the spot, the chief paused, and, pointing to the group, said:

"L'Espion Hardi is of the race of the paleface. It becomes him to look to the burial of his dead. See! the good blackgown is wrapt in sorrow! the words of the chief would disturb his spirit. The braves will bury their brothers!"

"Huron, I am but a rude forester. I have lived in the woods till I am like the Indian rather than my own blood and race"—

"Good!" said the chief, nodding his head approvingly; "Daring Scout is the brother of the Hurons!"

"Chief," continued Pierre, "the youth must be buried like a Christian white man."

"The Hurons are Christians," said the Indian slowly.

"True," replied the scout; "your brothers must not be turned into the earth like the heathen Mohawk! "We must bury them side by side with the youth!"

17   N

"Huron and pale-face—all the same in the ground—all the same before God!" said the chief earnestly.

"Not the same here on the earth though!" said the scout, clinging to the idea of the superiority of his race.

"No? Indian tell truth! Indian don't steal; he loves God and prays to him; what more pale-face?"

For a moment the scout was silent; at length he said: "True, Huron, but the pale face is richer and stronger; he builds splendid cities, makes fine houses, wears rich clothes, drinks costly wines." The scout ceased as he caught the meaning glance of the Huron's eye. But that look passed away in a moment, and Ahasistari said solemnly:

"What good all that—there and *there?*" as he pointed to the earth, and then to the sky. The scout was silent, and the chief, turning away, said: "Let us go!"

"Yes, it is time to dig their graves;" and the two entered the forest.

"It shall be," said Ahasistari, "where the foot of the Mohawk shall not tread upon them."

Selecting a suitable spot, the Huron and the Frenchman turned up the sod with their hatchets, and in a short time had scooped a resting-place for the dead. Then they retraced their steps to the village, and joined the group. Rude biers were made of the branches of trees strewed with the softest foliage, that the lifeless corpse might repose gently there. In one of the lodges had been found the sacks in which, slung upon their shoulders, the missionaries carried their vestments and the sacred vessels in their journeys through the boundless forests.

In his white surplice they robed the gentle novice; in that pure garment in which he had so often served at the holy sacrifice they wrapped him for the solemn burial. His hands were meekly crossed upon his breast. They raised him sadly, and laid him on his bier; they lifted it and strode forward.

At that instant a slight female figure pierced through the group, and gazed for a moment on the face of the dead. Then she placed a wreath of wild flowers upon his brow, and, starting away, the wail of the Indian girl arose for the departed.

Bearing torches in their hands, the procession wound solemnly into the forest, and paused beside the new-made grave. Slowly and carefully they laid him in his silent resting-place, while the light of the torches beamed upon his angelic face, and reflected from the glowing colors of the wild flowers on his brow, his cheek seemed to bloom with a tinge of life. He had passed into death suddenly, in the midst of prayer; its heavenly radiance still hovered around the chiselled features. Beautiful in death, crowned with the wreath of flowers, and robed in unspotted white, the young martyr lay, a halo of unearthly glory seeming to the rapt beholders already to glow around his brow. By the side of the gentle novice they stretched the scarred forms of the two Huron warriors. In silence their brothers laid them down to mingle their dust with one of another race, yet one in faith, and hope, and charity; one by the bond of that church which gathers alike all souls within her fold.

"De profundis clamavi ad te, Domine!" arose in the deep voice of the priest, and the Hurons responded.

O! how solemn was the burial ceremony there, in the hour of midnight, by the wild gleam of torches, under the forest-trees, with. the dusky forms of the Hurons grouped around the grave.

It was done. Upon the cold bosom of the dead fell the clodded earth, which was to be the dwelling-place and home of the body until its mouldering dust should mingle with it. Carefully they replaced each sod, and, above the whole, strewed the fallen leaves again so skilfully that it might never more be found save by those who now looked upon it. As they finished, a figure flitted from the spot; the Indian maiden had been gazing on the scene. In silence they wended their way back to the village, Ahasistari and Le Loup in the rear, covering every footstep, and removing every trace of their passage. When they had reached the centre of the village, the chief addressed the priest:

"Father, there is little time to spare; the routed Mohawks may reach the nearest villages of their tribe by daybreak, and we have many days' march before us!"

"I am ready, my son," said the Jesuit sadly,
17 *

for the death of his young companion weighed
heavily upon him. As he spoke, Morning
Flower stood before him, and, in a low tone,
mentioned the name of Kiskepila, and pointed
to his lodge. The Jesuit followed her thither,
while the Hurons made their preparations for
departure, gathering all the arms at the village,
and destroying them, and loading themselves
with a supply of corn for the march. Father
Laval found the young Indian stretched upon
his couch, his face covered with his hands.

"My son," he said, "be not cast down!"

The Indian looked up proudly; but the glow
of spirit passed in a moment from his cheek, and
he said:

"The home of Kiskepila is destroyed; his
people are slain, and he must lie upon his bed
helpless as a woman! Bid the Hurons come;
Kiskepila would die!"

At this moment Ahasistari entered, and stood
behind the Jesuit; all was ready for departure,
and time was pressing; but he waited patiently
till Father Laval should conclude his conversation. As soon as the Mohawk saw him, he

raised himself, and, with a look of proud defiance, said:

"Kiskepila is the young eagle of his tribe! the triumph of the Huron is but little without his scalp."

Ahasistári did not move; but the Jesuit replied: "My son, do not entertain such thoughts; the Huron does not desire to shed your blood. It is our sincerest wish to be your friend, and the friends of all men rather than their foes." The Huron chief assented.

After a pause, the Mohawk continued: "My people are routed; but they fled, not from the living, but from the dead! The blackgown called the great white warrior from the spirit-land to rescue him."

Father Laval listened in wonder, and replied: "My son, this is some wild mistake."

"Champlain!" said the other; "Kiskepila heard the cry, and saw the warriors of his tribe turn like women from the face of the white man. Who could fight the dead?"

In a moment the whole matter became apparent to the mind of the Jesuit. The division of

opinion in the village, in regard to the policy of
condemning so great a medicine as they considered Father Laval, had made the taunt of Kiohba
remembered; and when they heard the cry
"Champlain!" and saw the assault led on by a
white man, they believed that the challenge of
Kiohba had been accepted, and that the great
Frenchman had arisen from the tomb to the
rescue. Whilst the priest was endeavoring to
explain this to the Mohawk, Ahasistari left the
lodge, and in a few moments returned with
Pierre.

"L'Espion Hardi," he said. The Mohawk
looked upon the scout for a moment; then
hiding his head in his hands, remained in
imperturbable silence.

"Yes! L'Espion Hardi," said the scout,
"that's the name the Hurons call me, and, if I
had not been delayed in the swamp ground in
getting to my station according to the plan of
the chief; or, if he had held his fire a little
longer until I gave the signal, not a Mohawk
would have escaped."

"It is well," said the chief. "But L'Espion
Hardi was delayed in the forest too."

"Ah, your Huron nearly missed the trail, but
we came in time."

"Yes. Ahasistari was about to fulfil his oath,
and go to die with his father at the torture fire,
when the sounds of the coming braves struck
upon his ear."

Father Laval addressed a few kind words to
the Mohawk, and left the lodge. The Hurons
bound all those who were left at the village; and,
having heaped a mass of fuel upon the fires to
impress any returning stragglers with the idea
that a strong force was still there, leaving a
broad trail to the edge of the forest on the north-
west as if striking to the waters of Ontario, then
doubling and striking into its depth towards the
northeast, hastened rapidly on their return.

The time which must elapse before any pursuit
could begin would enable them to escape, provided Father Laval held out. The party under
Watook had, in order to be sure of the route of
the Mohawks, proceeded to the scene of the first
encounter, and had there found the canoes which
had been concealed in readiness for another foray.
With fortunate precaution Watook, after observ-

ing the direction of the trail, had sent these barks
up a stream which flowed into the St. Lawrence
from the Mohawk country. Several days' rapid
journeying, in which they sought little sleep or
rest, brought them to the spot where the boats
were concealed. Here they embarked, and descending quickly to the St. Lawrence, turned
their course once more with saddened and chastened hearts towards the Huron missions.

CHAPTER XII.

THE CONCLUSION.

YEARS passed. Twice had the snows of winter fallen; twice the blossoms of spring had bloomed: summer was upon the land; and the fields and waters laughed in glad sunshine.

It was at the close of day that a group of idlers, resting upon the quay at Quebec, gazed out listlessly upon the waters, observing the motions of the boats passing to and from the few vessels lying in the river. Occasionally a canoe, paddled by Indians, would shoot out from the shore, and pass gracefully along the waters, as its occupants bent their course towards their settlements; for the Christian Indians had formed themselves into communities, and lived around their churches and their priests — the

203

flock around the shepherd—within the borders
of the province.

"The Indians are returning to their homes,"
said one of the group. "I thought they would
have remained in town to-night; to-morrow is
the festival of the Assumption."

"True," said another; "but they are returning
to celebrate it at their own villages."

"They are very pious and devout," continued
the first. "Their example is enough to shame
the better instructed white."

"Better instructed!" said the second speaker
with a laugh; "but that depends upon the sense
in which you use the phrase. They are unsophisticated, it is true; and their pastors, the Jesuits,
have succeeded in preserving them from the con-
tamination which so often follows in the path of
the white man in his contact with the Indians.
They are untaught in the world's learning, perhaps, and undervalue it; but I warrant thee,
neighbor, they will repeat the Pater and the
Ave, and the creed and the decalogue, with thee,
and explain them too, as well as thou canst; and
what is better still, neighbor, they practise what

they have learned: a thing which you and I, and many more of the 'better instructed,' sometimes do not consider as necessary as we ought."

"Yes, I admit they are good and practical Christians—thanks to the zeal and energy and purity of life of their pastors."

"Is it not admirable, this courage and daring of the Jesuits, that led them into the forest to bring these wanderers to God?"

"They tell me," said another, "that in France there are some who begin to rail against the order as proud, intriguing—as seeking after wealth and power."

"Oh, doubtless! Yes, I have heard so, neighbor. They seek wealth in strange places; here in the forest, in China, in England on the scaffold. Yes, it is the wealth of heaven they are seeking! Ah, it would be a glorious thing to place one of these silken-robed revilers by the side of an humble Jesuit in the forest, beyond the great lakes, among the wild Indians, who have never yet seen the face of a white man. Give them both staff and scrip, and a wooden cross—"

18

"Aye, or bind them both to the stake, with the savage Iroquois around them, tearing their flesh and torturing them to death, as I have seen the Jesuit die, with a prayer upon his lips" — said a voice abruptly, and the speaker rose from a seat which he had occupied near the party, but concealed from them by some bales of goods, and turned his steps towards the town. A pause for a moment ensued.

"Who is that man?" asked one of the group.

"Ah, that is *L'Espion Hardi!*" said the defender of the Jesuits, whose name was Paul. "I have heard it said that he was out some years ago with a party of Hurons, who endeavored to rescue two missionaries from the Mohawks. It is a sad tale; but it so often happens thus in this wild land, that one can scarcely recall all the facts to mind. Yes, one they saved, Father Jean Laval; the other, a novice, was already dead at the torture-fire when they became master of the village. The Daring Scout is right; bind the Jesuit and his reviler to the stake, and see who will die with the sweetest conscience and the most placid smile — see whose soul will best befit a martyr. Ah! it is the hour of death which proves the value of the past life—which tries its motives, and explains and illustrates them. That is the hour when cunning is of no avail; when wrong will weigh upon the conscience, and wring out the cry of horror from the soul. The death of one Jesuit is worth the whole lives of a thousand of their revilers. The dying of the one, and the living of the other, alike, are irresistible arguments in behalf of the assailed and the reviled.*

"The blood-prints of their martyrs have already rendered holy the borders of New France, and sanctified and dedicated to God the great valley beyond the western lakes. They have bought it with their toils and sufferings!"

---

* Compare the dying scene of the Jesuit martyr in China, in Japan, amongst the Mohawks, or with Abenakis—even upon the scaffold in the realm of Britain—suffering in the dissemination of religion, in the teaching of morality, with the life of an enemy of theirs, such as *Sue*, spent in sowing broadcast the seed of immorality and licentiousness, in spreading infidelity, in assailing Christianity, and battening upon sin and sorrow. Ah, it is glorious to have *such* enemies; they are their own refutation, their own condemnation, with all rational Christians.

"And this *L'Espion Hardi*—I have never seen him before — does he come often to Quebec?"

"It is very plain that you are not long of New France. Of late he comes frequently for ammunition, as he says: but he always calls at the house of the Jesuits: for during that event he formed a reverential affection towards the patient and enduring priest, which the rude hunter cannot conquer."

"Then Father Laval is still here?"

"Yes," said M. Paul; "he returned from the Huron missions some months since, and is recruiting his health, which was much shattered by the incessant toils and labors of a two years' mission among the wandering tribes, added to the effects of the sufferings he endured while in captivity among the Mohawks. But see! yonder come two canoes down the river towards the city; all that we have hitherto observed were leaving it."

The rest of the group directed their eyes up the river upon the objects indicated. Sweeping majestically around that point from which Father Laval had bid adieu to Quebec two years before,

came two canoes, each urged by several rowers.
Aided by the current, they rapidly neared the
town, until it was possible to distinguish the
faces of the occupants. In the first canoe stood
a young Indian of powerful frame. His head
was ornamented with eagle-feathers; his dress
was a rich robe of skins, bound round his waist
with a finely worked belt; his face was free from
paint, and he was totally unarmed. Behind
him rowed another Indian, the cross around
whose neck proclaimed him to be a Christian.
The second canoe contained a single male and
two females; one youthful and beautiful, in
whom the freshness of girlhood had ripened
into fuller bloom. The other was older, and
the hand of time had already scattered a few
white hairs among her thick locks. At the
bow of each canoe was fastened a green branch,
the Indian symbol of peace and amity. The
young warrior paused for a moment to gaze
upon the growing city, and then bending again
to his paddle, sent the light bark on more fleetly.
The evening sun was still casting his glory upon
the waters, when the bow of the first canoe

18 *   O

grated on the sand of the quay below the lookers-on. The Indian warrior leaped ashore, and his companion drew the light bark upon the beach. In another moment the whole party stood together. Then the Christian Indian taking the lead, at a quick pace turned towards the town. It was too common a sight in Quebec to attract any extraordinary attention, and the party passed on unheeded. The young brave of the eagle feathers trod on in silence, scarce deigning to notice what to him must have been wondrous wealth and opulence, but regardless of all around he followed in the lead of his guide. At length the Christian Indian, a Huron, paused before a house of some size, and after looking about, as if to recognize the landmarks of the place, advanced to the door and knocked. In a few moments it was opened.

"A Huron captive from the Mohawks," he said to the janitor, "would see his father of the blackgown." The door was cast open, and they entered. After a little delay the superior came to them.

"My son, what is it that you wish?" he said to the Huron.

"My father," he replied, pointing to the young brave, "a Mohawk neophyte."

Long did the good old Jesuit gaze upon the powerful young Mohawk, one of that terrible race of Iroquois who had hitherto resisted the efforts of the missionary, and now heaven had sent one to his door demanding admission to the church.

"Yes; there is but one," he said, speaking half aloud, "who can speak the Mohawk and Huron tongue; and though in ill health, he is full of zeal. Stay," he continued aloud, "my children. I will send one to you who can speak your own language," and left the room.

The Mohawk remained cold and imperturbable, evincing no curiosity as to what had been said, or anxiety for the result, though he had closely watched the face of the speaker. The females of the party were not as impassive, but examined with wonder the simple decorations of the reception room, looking with astonishment upon the few plain pictures which adorned the walls. At length a step was heard without; and, through the opened door, entered a Jesuit. His face was averted as he came in, but when he had closed the door he advanced towards them. It was Father Laval. His countenance was very pale and attenuated, and his hair was gray: for the toils of a few such years as his had been will touch with white, as surely as the placid flow of many. Suddenly the impassive face of the Mohawk warrior lit up with a bright smile; a low exclamation of surprise broke from his lips, and he stepped forward to a spot where, from a window, the light fell full upon his manly form, and said:

" Blackgown! — Kiskepila! — Morning Flower!"

The Jesuit clasped his hands, and looked towards heaven, for the memory of sad scenes came over his soul; but in a moment the cloud passed, and joyously he stretched out his hands:

" Welcome, Young Eagle! Welcome, gentle maiden! Sad were the scenes in which we parted; joyful is this hour in which you come back to me, like the fruit of my captivity."

The Indian maiden wept as she took the hand of the priest, and she said : " In spring-time and in summer, Morning Flower has strewed fresh flowers over the grave of the young pale-face; and she has prayed there that the God of the pale-face would hear her. She has said, often — often : ' Mary ! Mary ! ' "

" And heaven has heard your prayer ! " exclaimed the priest.

" Kiskepila has thought many times upon the words of the blackgown," said the young Mohawk; and pointing to the Huron captive, he continued : " Kiskepila took the Huron captive : and he told him over and over the teaching of the good father, that he might not forget it. The Mohawks are at war with the French; but the Mohawk brave has come hither to be baptized. Kiodego has gone to the spirit-land, and Kiskepila is a chief in his village. Morning Flower often talked of the teaching of the blackgown, and would seek the father of the pale-face. She has come with the mother of Kiskepila."

Father Laval learned that the Indian maiden,

cherishing his instructions in her memory, and gaining further knowledge from the Huron captive, had refused to become the wife of the chief, except through the Christian sacrament: and to be received into the church the party had undertaken the long journey to Quebec. Kiskepila informed the priest that, after the surprise at the village and the departure of the victors, the Mohawks had not reassembled until late the next day; that then a strong party, with reinforcements from the other villages, had set out in pursuit, but that after an ineffectual chase had returned, having lost the trail upon the banks of a stream of water that flowed into the St. Lawrence; that he had explained away to them the cause of their panic, and had ever after maintained an ascendancy among them, and led them on as their favorite war-chief.

Father Laval then began to question the two neophytes upon the subject of religion. He found their dispositions good, and their instruction, so far as it had gone, solid and well understood; and, after consulting with his superior, determined that they should be baptized on the

morrow, as an offering to God, through the
Virgin, on the feast of the Assumption, and
as a dedication of the nation of the Iroquois
to Christ under her invocation. Accordingly
he placed the two females under the protection
of the nuns of the Ursuline convent, with
directions that the maiden should be further
instructed and prepared, by means of an inter-
preter, for the reception of baptism and the
sacrament of penance. In their own house
Kiskepila and his two companions were shel-
tered — Father Laval that same evening attend-
ing the necessary preparations on the part of
the young chief.

With the dawn of morning rung out the
joyous peals of the church-bells for the festival
of the Assumption. The city was thronged;
many of the colonists from the country had
assembled to celebrate the festival in the capital.
Crowds of strangers and Indians filled the
streets. The military, in all the pomp and
circumstance of war, were drawn out in long
array, preparatory to marching to the cathedral
to assist at the holy sacrifice. At length the

pealing bells again rung out, the solemn chant
arose in the holy temple, the deep-toned organ
swelled up its lengthened aisles. All Quebec
had gathered there, for the rumor had gone
forth that an interesting ceremony was to be
performed at the conclusion of the bishop's
solemn mass. The hour came. Kneeling at
the baptistery, before the sacred font, were two
figures—an Indian warrior and a female. Over
the head of the latter was thrown a light veil of
muslin, through which her jet-black hair showed
its glossy hue. She was clothed in a neat dress
of spotless white. Beyond them knelt a crowd
of mingled colonists and natives. Beside the
sacred font stood up the Jesuit, Father Laval,
enrobed, and holding his missal in his hands.
On either side were acolytes, with lighted tapers
in their hands. The ceremony proceeded; it
was finished; and with extended hands the
priest bestowed upon them his blessing. The
neophytes arose. In solemn procession they
moved towards the altar. The priest entered
within the sanctuary, and they stood before him.
He joined their hands; he placed the sacred

ring upon the finger of the maiden; he uttered the final blessing of the church upon those who worthily enter into the holy bonds of matrimony, and the affecting scene was ended. Tears gathered in the eyes of Father Laval as he uttered the last prayer. Two years ago that very day, upon the feast of the Assumption, he had run the gauntlet in the villages of the Mohawk. These two young souls were now before him, the first fruits of his toils and sufferings, through the merits of Christ, and he returned thanks to God for his goodness in sending him so abundant consolation. At this moment a Huron pressed through the kneeling crowd, advanced towards the Mohawk, and stretching out his hands, exclaimed:

"Kiskepila! there has been war between thy people and my people. Let the hatchet be buried. Let the tree of peace spring up, and the Mohawk and the Huron will rest together, like brothers, under its shade. It is the spirit of the religion which thou hast embraced."

"The words of the chief of the Hurons are good! Kiskepila loveth peace! He has come

19

unarmed into the fortress of his brothers. The blackgown has taught Kiskepila that they are the lovers of peace, the merciful, and the forgiving, who are to be happy!" and the young Mohawk grasped the hand of Ahasistari.

"The lion and the lamb shall lie down together—it is true; the Mohawk and the Huron are friends," said a voice, and the figure of L'Espion Hardi was seen passing down the aisle of the cathedral with a sad and pensive step.

Together the two chiefs knelt before the altar, and with uplifted hands the priest besought blessings from heaven on the union, and peace thus made and cemented by the solemnities of his holy church.

"O God! I thank thee for thy ineffable goodness to thy unworthy servant!" exclaimed the Jesuit as he departed from the church with a happy heart. "Thou didst turn my steps from the beaten path to those who had already heard thy Gospel, to tread in sorrow and captivity the way to the darkened heathen; and thou didst there make me plant in sadness and suffering the seed which has this day, through thy grace, borne fruit in peace and joy. Thou guidest our steps and directest our energies. Truly out of seeming evil thou dost bring forth good."

In that year a solemn treaty of peace was formed between the French and the Iroquois, and a mission was founded in the Mohawk valley. And although interrupted by outbreaks of the savages, and interrupted by wars, it constantly revived, until at a period of ten years later, "there, in the heart of New York, the solemn services of the Roman Catholic church were chanted as securely as in any part of Christendom." *

* Bancroft, III. p. 113.